WRITING
TOOLS

for the

COLLEGE
ADMISSIONS
ESSAY

OTHER BOOKS BY ROY PETER CLARK

Writing Tools: 55 Essential Strategies for Every Writer

Tell It Like It Is: A Guide to Clear and Honest Writing

Murder Your Darlings: And Other Gentle Writing Advice from Aristotle to Zinsser

The Art of X-Ray Reading: How the Secrets of 25 Great Works of Literature Will Improve Your Writing

How to Write Short: Word Craft for Fast Times

Help! for Writers: 210 Solutions to the Problems Every Writer Faces

The Glamour of Grammar: A Guide to the Magic and Mystery of Practical English

WRITING TOOLS

TOOLS

for the

COLLEGE ADMISSIONS ESSAY

WRITE YOUR WAY INTO THE
SCHOOL OF YOUR DREAMS

ROY PETER CLARK

LITTLE, BROWN SPARK
New York Boston London

Little, Brown Spark
Hachette Book Group
1290 Avenue of the Americas, New York, NY 10104
littlebrownspark.com

First Edition: May 2025

Little, Brown Spark is an imprint of Little, Brown and Company, a division of Hachette Book Group, Inc. The Little, Brown Spark name and logo are trademarks of Hachette Book Group, Inc.

The publisher is not responsible for websites (or their content) that are not owned by the publisher.

The Hachette Speakers Bureau provides a wide range of authors for speaking events. To find out more, go to hachettespeakersbureau.com or email HachetteSpeakers@hbgusa.com.

Little, Brown and Company books may be purchased in bulk for business, educational, or promotional use. For information, please contact your local bookseller or the Hachette Book Group Special Markets Department at special.markets@hbgusa.com.

ISBN 9780316567671
LCCN 2024944360

Printing 1, 2025

LSC-C

Printed in the United States of America

This book is dedicated to my writing students over fifty years — from young children to seasoned professionals. Thank you for teaching me how to grow as a writer, a teacher, and a person.

Contents

From this section you can learn:

* The shape, length, and key parts of a successful essay
* How an essay can be a story, and how the best stories work
* How stories can reveal your character, intelligence, and values

From this section you can learn:

* How to decide what should come first in your essay
* The value of placing something cool — or hot! — at the beginning of your story

* What it takes to write a good lead, a first move that hooks the reader and captures the focus of the story
* The writer always has choices — not necessarily good or bad — about ways to influence the reader.

From this section you can learn:

* The most common prompts used by colleges and universities
* How to choose among a variety of prompts
* How to find that special object that has a story hiding within
* What it means to overcome an obstacle, and why this makes for a great story
* How to transform the topic within a prompt into a story that only you can write

From this section you can learn:

* Good writing is not magic but the result of a process, a set of steps.
* Focus is central to the process.
* There are things you can do when you get stuck.
* Rehearsal is the antidote to procrastination.

From this section you can learn:

* Tools of originality to help you avoid the unethical borrowing of other people's work
* Strategies of writing and research that help you overcome the temptation to make things up

* The most helpful and most honest way to deal with writing chatbots and other digital tools
* Creating and presenting the most authentic version of yourself

From this section you can learn:

* What we mean when we talk about a writer's "voice"
* Strategies to help you modulate your voice and influence the reader's experience
* How to write so you sound like yourself—or a little better
* The value of reading your work aloud
* How to read your own work and others' with your eyes and ears

From this section you can learn:

* How various writers solve the problems presented by a list of prompts
* What diversity looks like within a creative group of young writers
* How to appreciate a good essay
* How to recognize ways a good essay might become better

From this section you can learn:

* Tips and tricks the best writers use to do their best work

* How to use these writing strategies more purposefully
* How to build a workbench to store all your tools, now and into the future

IX. The Power of Revision 163

From this section you can learn:

* The differences between revision and proofreading
* Strategies for taking a good essay and making it better
* The ability to recognize what works in your essay and what needs work
* How questions from a coach, or questions you ask yourself about a draft, can lead to something better

X. Learn and Inspire 209

From this section you can learn:

* What a truly great student essay looks like
* How the best coaches work — help you can share with parents and teachers

Ways to Read This Book

FOR HIGH SCHOOL STUDENTS

If you are holding this book in your hands, know that it was written with your needs in mind. Perhaps you are a junior or senior in high school. You hope or plan to go to college. You may have a few schools in mind, and you want to give yourself the best chance to get accepted. The more competitive the school, the more important the personal essay becomes.

This book has been designed and written to be as helpful as possible. You will find many strategies writers use to create their best work. You will find many diverse examples of effective essays, with commentary on what makes them good. Most important, you will find encouragement, not just on this important task, but on your ability to think of yourself, maybe for the first time, as a writer.

FOR ADVANCED STUDENTS AND PROFESSIONALS

Beyond getting into college, you may need to write an essay when applying for higher degrees. I have coached students who want to get into law school, medical school, and graduate programs in a variety of disciplines. I myself once had to write an essay to apply for a prestigious fellowship. (I didn't get it.)

Perhaps you work for a nonprofit and are applying for a grant to win resources for your project. Or you want to publish your own book and need to write a book proposal that includes a story about who you are. Don't be put off by the words *high school* on the title page. Every tool a high school junior needs to write a good essay will also help you, including the steps of the writing process and the most powerful elements of storytelling. Dive in.

FOR TEACHERS, TUTORS, AND COACHES

Thank you for finding this book. It will give you many tools for helping students create the effective essays that only they can write. Good writing is not magic. It's a process, with a set of steps you can share with your students.

It is one thing to teach a young writer about some element of language or rhetoric. How you teach it matters — a lot. That is why we have included tips on how to be a good writing coach. The effective writing teacher asks good questions — and listens. That teacher also reads a draft of an essay to discover its unfulfilled potential: what works and what needs work.

It's your job to invite your students inside that lifelong club where reading and writing hold special importance.

FOR PARENTS

I am a parent myself, so I know you have the most difficult task of all: giving your student the room they need to write the essay that only they can write — in an authentic voice that is truly theirs and not yours.

That said, it will be good for you to explore this book for strategies that you can apply in your own reading and writing. While we ask you not to write the essay for your student and not to mark up an early draft in red ink, we also point you to many ways that you can help.

If a student chooses to write about the day they were born, for example, you can answer questions to enrich their experiences. You can encourage them to get started, but please don't strap them into their chairs and stand over them to make sure they stay on task.

Encourage, love, support, share, answer — in other words, offer good examples on what it means to become an effective and honest writer.

Write Your Way In

I wonder, as I write this, what I could tell you about myself that would help you think highly of me. Perhaps I could list my achievements: the books I have published and the honors I have received. Or, perhaps, I could tell you a small story, just five hundred words, or maybe only three hundred.

I could tell you how I rescued a feral cat, named Duchess, and have taken care of her every day for ten years.

You might like to hear about how I discovered my mom's last surviving cousin of her thirty-five first cousins and what I learned about their shared family history.

Or I could write about how I was sixteen years old when the Beatles came to America, and the only thing I wanted to do was play in a rock band. (I have, for more than sixty years.)

I have written about all these topics in a type of story called the personal essay. Just because it is personal does not mean that it has to be all about you. It can be about something or someone you know well—something or someone that is particularly meaningful to you. For example, you could write about the destruction of that old house down the street that you used to play in. You could write about the mail carrier who never seemed to miss a day of work and who knew you by name, or that movie that you have watched forty-seven times.

In one sense, it may not matter which topic you choose, as long as it passes this test: It opens up a window through which a reader can discover your values and virtues: who you are, how you think, and what you would add to the academic and cultural life of the school you are applying to.

No one taught me how to write a personal essay. I learned by reading and enjoying them. As I came to understand more about the writing process, I began to recognize some of the strategies used by the best storytellers and essayists. I am writing this book to share those tips and tools with you. I hope you will use this knowledge to write the best story about yourself that you've ever written. The story only you can write.

Your goal may be to write an essay that will help get you in the college of your choice, or the grad school of your choice, or maybe the internship or job you've always dreamed of. If you don't think of yourself as a writer, put your worries aside. You don't need to have straight A's in your English classes or be on the staff of the school newspaper to think of yourself as a writer. Anyone who writes anything gets to call themselves a writer. I call myself a golfer and a musician, not because I am Tiger Woods or Jimi Hendrix, but because I knock the little white ball around and play the keyboard in a garage band.

Chances are you have never yet had any training in how to write the personal essay. I have coached high school students and teachers for more than four decades. I love working with them, but I am always surprised that schools don't place more emphasis on teaching the personal essay. I say that because writing your college admissions essay may turn out to be the highest-stakes piece of writing you ever create. And personal writing is a skill that you can take with you to college — and beyond.

I applied to college in 1965. I was salutatorian at a prestigious Catholic high school on Long Island; I was a class officer with several other extracurricular activities; I played in a rock band named T.S. and the Eliots. I took the SAT exam just once and scored a combined 1320. Maybe that was a little low, because I didn't get into Princeton University, my dream school. I wish I could read my college essay now.

That's the cool thing about the admissions essay. By the end of your junior year in high school, there is little you can do to raise your grades and your GPA. You could do some volunteer work to show your civic spirit. You can take the ACT or SAT exam more than once to bump up your score. Not every college requires an essay, but for those that do, it is your final chance to impress the jury. I was a good student but not a great taker of standardized tests. (I think it was because I liked to linger over verbal and logical questions.) If you are not the Master of Tests, fear not. A good essay might carry you over the line.

Over the years, I have talked to members of the essay "jury": admissions officers of an excellent private school in St. Petersburg, Florida: Eckerd College. Their testimony was quite striking. They revealed to me that they tended to divide essays into three categories, which I will describe as the 10/60/30 percent ratio. That means that 10 percent of the essays were so bad, so thoughtless, so riddled with mistakes (sometimes including the misspelling of the name of the school) that the officers wanted to ban the student from the campus. As for the majority, the 60 percent, those essays all sounded so similar, so plain, so generic that you could throw them up in the air, catch one, and it would read like all the others.

That leaves the final 30 percent. These stood out for their care, creativity, and the compelling story they told about the writer. You can imagine how many essays these readers have to process and how quickly they must be dispatched. These were the essays that readers wanted to linger over and immediately share with the other readers.

An excellent student at Elon College in North Carolina just sent me the essay she wrote in high school. It was a good essay but not a great one. The writer told the story of her pin collection. In her travels, she would buy a pin that signified some new place. She would then attach the pin to a burlap tote her mother had given her. A bland, rough bag became a sparkling representation of her adventures. Here's the key point: Even though the essay probably didn't rank in the top 10 percent, it still managed to help her get accepted into thirteen of the fifteen schools to which she applied. So relax.

That said, I encourage you to shoot for the top. You can get there with the coaching you receive from this book.

Imagine an essay that starts with the line "I want to be an English major at your school because I have always enjoyed reading." Now imagine that same essay started with this line instead: "Picture me at nine years old, under the covers with a flashlight, ignoring video games and reading how a giant squid entangled a submarine in *Twenty Thousand Leagues Under the Sea.*"

What is that difference? The first is easily forgettable. It could be about anyone. The second gives its readers something to remember. It's a story that sets the writer apart, a story about a specific person in a specific moment.

PART I

The Essay Only You Can Write

From this section you can learn:

* The shape, length, and key parts of a successful essay
* How an essay can be a story, and how the best stories work
* How stories can reveal your character, intelligence, and values

WHAT A GOOD PERSONAL ESSAY LOOKS LIKE

When you sit down at the keyboard with a blank screen, try not to worry about creating the "perfect essay." That may cause unnecessary anxiety. At the beginning of the process, it actually helps you to lower your standards, knowing that you have a chance to make a draft of your story better and better with each revision. Let's get your essay to "good," not perfect, and build from there.

To help you see what a good essay looks like, I will be offering you one of my favorites, from a young man I've known since he was a toddler. His name is Sam French. At thirty-two, he currently lives in New York City, and works as a playwright, screenwriter, and director.

He wrote this essay years ago as an honor student at a high school in St. Petersburg, Florida, which had a magnet program in performing arts. I was beginning to collect examples of student work, and Sam generously shared what you are about to read.

Lonesome George

By Sam French

(452 words)

I didn't speak any Spanish. She spoke a little English. What could possibly go wrong? I was an American high school tourist in the Galapagos Islands. She was a beautiful young Ecuadorean woman working in a snorkel shop. It was like *West Side Story*, only with less singing and knife-fighting.

I liked her instantly. I liked the way she smiled. I liked her voice. I liked that she was wearing a *Nightmare*

Before Christmas T-shirt that would be considered uncool at my school. I liked her mystique. I liked the way that she didn't have a calculator and had to figure out the customer's change in her head. That was hot. I liked that she worked at a snorkel shop. I liked the word "snorkel." I liked it all.

Admittedly, I was out of my element. Usually, when I tried to talk to a pretty girl, I was in America, my home turf. I wondered if on the Galapagos Islands, flirting was any different. The male great frigatebirds, indigenous to the islands, attract females by puffing out a red pouch on their neck, demonstrating their ultimate masculinity. I realized that if I were to woo her, I would need to put my best traits on display. Like the great frigatebird, I would have to puff out my metaphorical red pouch thingy.

Normally, I would have been too afraid to talk to her, but this summer was different. This was a summer for taking risks. I felt adventurous, invincible—like James Bond. This was the summer I pierced my ear and ate guinea pig. This summer, I couldn't be stopped. Maybe I would make a fool out of myself. Maybe, like Icarus, I would fly too close to the sun. But this was Ecuador, not Greece, and I felt strangely awesome.

My friends tried to dissuade me. "She's too pretty for you." "Are you kidding me?" "You're pathetic." Doubt began to creep in. Staring at her from across the room, I started to second-guess myself. What if she didn't like

me? What if I sounded like an idiot? What did I have to
offer that the average Ecuadorean teenage male didn't?
She probably had a boyfriend who looked like me but
was exotic and good at soccer. I almost turned around
and walked away. But I stopped. Down the street, at the
Charles Darwin Research Center, was a tortoise named
Lonesome George. George is lonesome because he is
the only known Pinta Island tortoise left alive. George is
lonesome because he will never be able to have a mate
that he truly belongs with. I glanced at the girl, glanced
at my friends, and walked toward her. This one's for you,
Lonesome George.

I remember the first time I read this essay. I was struck at how
offbeat it seemed, nothing at all like what I imagined an essay
could be. My instinct was to share it widely, with other students
and teachers, with other professional writers and editors.
People laughed when I read it aloud. Almost everyone
said that if they were admissions officers at a college, they
would want Sam French on their campus — and clearly the
admissions office at Carnegie Mellon University in Pittsburgh
felt the same way when they accepted him into the elite program
in theater directing.

When the ancient tortoise Lonesome George eventually
died, the *Tampa Bay Times* reprinted Sam's essay on its
op-ed page.

I am not arguing that it is a perfect essay. But let's focus
on the elements that have made it attractive to readers:

1. **It is short.** Your instructions may call for an essay of 1,000 words, or 750, or 500, or 300. Sam's essay comes in at about 450 words. Too often in writing, we equate excellence with length, as if a six-hundred-page novel must be somehow more important than a sixty-page novella. But throughout history, we have example after example of short works that have the deepest meaning. They are more memorable because they are short. Add up the words in the Hippocratic Oath, any Shakespeare sonnet, the parable of the Good Samaritan, the Preamble to the Constitution, and the Gettysburg Address, and you will be amazed to find that, all together, they total fewer than one thousand words.

   My personal habit is to ignore length at first. Among writers, I am called a putter-inner. I write to whatever length feels comfortable without filters, to say whatever it is I want to say. That "zero draft" (so named because it's not yet a first draft) tells me what I already know. It can also teach me my focus. If it does, then, through revision, I can cut it down to size.

2. **It transports the reader.** Not all effective essays are stories. But stories do have a special power. Let's call that power "transportation." In fewer than five hundred words, Sam transports us to another time and another place. Stories can be like time machines. A Wikipedia page may inform you about the Galapagos Islands, but Sam puts you there. He uses some of the most reliable methods of storytelling. He has characters. They exist in a place we

call a setting. He has enough room to create a scene, something we might see on Netflix. There is a bit of dialogue. And there is a chronology that invites us to follow along. He also creates a story engine, a question raised at the beginning that can be answered only by reading the story: "Will this young man find the courage to approach an attractive young woman from another country?" It is not "Who done it?" or "Guilty or not guilty?" but it is effective in a romantic comedy kind of way.

3. **It has vivid details**. Details show you things that can appeal to the senses. Most of Sam's details describe the young woman who has piqued his interest. The movie title on her T-shirt is a detail that helps define character. So is the fact that she does not use a calculator to make change. As for Sam himself, he reveals that he has a pierced ear and once ate guinea pig, as evidence of his daring personality. If details are about people, they add up and lead us to opinions and feelings about the characters in a story.

4. **It has a voice.** I can almost hear the author reading this essay on a public radio broadcast. It has personality, heart, and energy. I have read it aloud, and it flows easily as a story. Not all essays I have read aloud work this way. I often stumble because of bumps in the text, obstacles that the writer may not see but that someone reading aloud can hear.

5. **It shines a light on the writer's knowledge.** When writing for any audience — and an audience of college

admissions officers in particular — you want those read-ers to say to themselves, "That's so smart," or "That writer is so clever." To come across as well-rounded, you want them to know that you are tuned into high culture and low, from Shakespeare to reality TV. Reread Sam's story and see all the things that he knows about: musical the-ater, James Bond, Greek mythology — and let's not forget the animals of the Galapagos and a bit of evolutionary biology. The things or people you name, remember, are your backup singers.

6. **It reveals certain characteristics that are virtuous.** When I read a personal essay, I often make a list of virtues or values that it reveals. These can come in adjective form. Sam is intelligent, curious, adventurous, well educated, in tune with popular culture. He is probably well-read, as evidenced by his vocabulary. He is also self-deprecating — that is, he does not take himself too seriously. It never feels as if he is bragging. He has friends, it seems, who know him well enough to challenge him. If you ask me, I want him at my school.

7. **It names things.** One way to find interesting language is to name things. Look at all the names in this short essay, Galapagos, *West Side Story*, the great frigatebird, James Bond, Icarus, and, the star of the show, Lonesome George. These make the story more interesting and make the writer seem more curious and tuned-up. There is a countermove, in which Sam does not know the name of the red pouch on the bird. He calls it his "metaphorical

red pouch thingy," which shows both humor and knowledge of rhetoric (he wants to come across as a regular person; few people would know the name of the pouch). The goal is to find language and use the best language to appeal to the reader.

8. **The writer has a sense of humor.** Humor is a universal lubricant. It can reduce the friction of unfamiliarity or high-stakes anxiety or obnoxious erudition. You can be sure that the reader of your essay has read countless others that take themselves too seriously. These essays tend to be boring.

   If essayists make me laugh — not at them, but with them — as Sam French did, I will probably want them in my college. I am especially attracted to humor that is self-deprecating, where the author is laughing a little at himself or herself. In regular newspaper columns, I write about myself (a lot) and my wife. I make fun of myself, of her, and of our lives together. For example, I am not the greatest driver in the world (but I am an excellent parallel parker). Karen got so tired of criticizing each act of my bad driving that she made a long list of my problems and assigned each one of them a number. "Eleven!" she would exclaim if I failed to switch off my turn signal after changing lanes. Or "Seventeen!" if she noticed I was driving too slowly.

   You may be saying to yourself, "But I am not a funny writer." Don't worry, there are lots of ways to inject humor, including by quoting the witticisms of others. I did not write, "Nothing succeeds like excess." It was Oscar Wilde, and he said it or wrote it more than a century ago. But I get to quote him.

9. **The writer matches the essay to his academic interests**. It should not surprise anyone who reads Sam's story that he would flourish in an elite academic theater program. Or that he is one of those rare theater people who has built a career from his passion. Sure, there is a little bit of Darwin in the essay. But there is more about movies, and the essay showcases the writer's gift for storytelling and scene construction. I know of a young man who wanted to study math at an Ivy League school. There were no theater references in his essay. Instead, he told the funny story of how he and a geeky friend in the fifth grade would argue over "whether zero was the halfway number between negative infinity and positive infinity." He was admitted to Brown.

10. **The writer takes us on a journey.** Readers enjoy accompanying writers on their journeys. Every novel I have read, every movie I have watched has taken me on a journey. That is what I mean when I say that a story is a form of transportation. We can go back in time and suffer through the Depression in *The Grapes of Wrath* by John Steinbeck. Or we can visit a dystopian future in George Orwell's *1984*. It is no different with Sam French, who takes us with him to Ecuador and the Galapagos Islands

for a whimsical romantic dream. This is important: You don't need to travel to South America to create a good story. I have written columns about a journey to the mall, to a baseball stadium, to a concert, to a museum, to a pool hall, and to a house down the block. We journey every day, and many of those experiences can be rendered in a story.

MY FAVORITE ESSAY OF ALL TIME

I am about to introduce you to one of my favorite student essays. Maybe my absolute favorite. There is a story behind it. Over many years, I have worked with a public school teacher named Holly Slaughter. She is an expert on teaching reading and writing, a published author, and a leader for teachers at the elementary school level. Holly has two daughters, and the younger one, Emme, was working on her college admissions essay. She wanted to join her older sister at the University of Florida. Now Holly knows how to coach writers of all ages, but as sometimes happens in families, Emme preferred not to be coached by her mom. That's where I came in.

Emme sent me a draft of her story. I read it once; I read it again, thinking of ways I might help her improve the draft. I read it a third time. Then I messaged Emme and her mom. "It's perfect," I told them. "I have no changes to suggest. If UF reads this and does not accept you, you don't want to be there."

What was all the hubbub about? See if this essay excites you as much as it did me.

She Wants to Be an Astrophysicist: Get Used to It

By Emme Slaughter

(650 words)

Two years ago, I won my family's Fantasy Football League. To many this may not seem like a highly esteemed accomplishment. But if you were to ask me how I felt, I would have told you I won the actual Super Bowl.

I eagerly began to count down the days until Christmas, excited not for the holiday itself, but instead because I would get to see my entire family gathered at one long dinner table. Put in more accurate terms, I would be surrounded by people who had all just suffered defeat to the youngest member of the family. I was ecstatic.

My whole life, I had spent every Sunday and Monday night sitting on the very edge of my couch with my dad, ready to leap out of my seat and cheer at any play that gained over 30 yards. I memorized all the penalties, all my favorite players' names, and became my mom's favorite person to ask when she got a football question on her Sunday crossword.

So, when I walked into Nana and Poppa's on

Christmas with a big grin on my face, exuberant to talk about my team's flawless fantasy season, I was not expecting the response from my oldest cousin, Josh: "How could we get beaten by a girl?" My heart sank as ripples of laughter, mostly from my boy cousins and uncles, echoed throughout the room.

While my response to Josh should have been a confident "Get used to it," my fifteen-year-old self could not muster a word. I tried to hold back tears. Was I embarrassed? And why? I now know that what I was feeling was shame, rooted in the message that a woman could never be more knowledgeable than a man at football, or anything for that matter.

The way that I view the world changed on that day. I became heightened in my awareness of gender roles and societal perceptions, especially as I explored my future in STEM. In my AP physics class, I couldn't help but notice that I was part of a very small portion of girls in a male-dominated class.

Between freshman and sophomore year, I was invited to attend an engineering camp at a state university. Excited, I listened to the camp leaders share the agenda for the week, including all kinds of engineering activities and competitions. We would build marshmallow launchers, attend lectures, and kick off the camp with the ultimate competition: science trivia.

I remember looking around the room and noticing

the majority of male students. I found myself allowing the implicit message to seep into my brain: boys are naturally better than girls at science. Wasn't the very make-up of the room showing me just that? I blocked out everything and focused on answering the questions at break-neck speed. Later, when I held the pineapple-shaped trivia championship trophy above my head, all of my fellow campers, boys and girls, were screaming and cheering me on.

Today, I have taken Marie Curie as my role model, and just as she did, I strive to be the best in everything I do regardless of whom I compete against. Curie discovered radium. She observed that radiation wasn't dependent on the organization of atoms at a molecular level; something was happening inside the atom itself. The atom is not inert, indivisible, or solid.

Like Curie's discovery, something has happened inside me, deeper than the molecular level. There have been times that I have been shaken and so unsure of myself that I was unwilling to speak. And times when I have felt indivisible and unstoppable. I am growing to understand that it does not matter whether I am attempting to succeed in a career dominated by men, because my mind and actions are completely independent of those around me. For those who doubt me along the way, I say, just wait and see. And get used to it.

THINGS I LOVE ABOUT THIS ESSAY

It's the essay only Emme could write.

It has a catchy title. This essay has a title and a brief subtitle, both of which tell us something about the writer. If you have a catchy title that attracts the interest of the reader and also captures the main message of the essay, you are in great shape. Notice that her desire to become an astrophysicist is never mentioned in the story. But she doesn't have to because that title is like something on a billboard or a movie house marquee. The title tells, and the story shows. Meanwhile, the subtitle, "Get used to it," is a brilliant use of a catchphrase that expresses the strong voice of the writer. Notice that she uses it three times — which in writing is always a magic number. She uses it in the subtitle, in the middle, and then again at the end. You plant it, you water it, you harvest it.

It has spirit. Sam's story had a playful spirit. Emme's essay has spirit, too, from first word to last. Sam is a romantic. Emme is a warrior princess, someone who is determined, indefatigable (which means she is tireless!) with her eyes on the prize. She has heart, which she displays in the most casual settings, and the most serious ones.

It has a focus. One way to tell if an essay has focus is to try to summarize the meaning in as few words as possible. She does the trick with the title, but supports it throughout: "I am a determined young woman whose vocation is to work in a field now dominated by boys and men. It doesn't matter if you approve or not. Here I come."

It reveals her character and her knowledge base. When I read the essay, I drew immediate conclusions about what kind of person the writer is. From the evidence of the text, I would use these adjectives: intelligent, curious, determined, focused, versatile, sensitive, clever, organized, and literate. She could have referenced Shakespeare rather than Madame Curie, but she makes the good decision to reveal the knowledge base she wanted to pursue. And it gets brainier and brainier. In that sense our author, intelligent throughout these 650 words, reveals her intelligence in stages. It is obvious that colleges and universities want to accept brainy young people, and the readers of this essay will get a good insight into what this student already knows and what kind of learner she is likely to be.

Its use of detail

It has vivid scenes. The first scene is at a family Christmas dinner, where the boys shame each other for losing to a girl. It includes that snippet of dialogue. Her disappointment in that moment is neutralized in the second scene where she lifts the trophy. I love the fact that she includes the detail that the trophy is shaped like a pineapple.

It shows and it tells. In kindergarten, I learned the game show-and-tell. I would bring in an object from home and tell the class a story about it. Never did I think that it would lead to a lesson I would use in my writing for a lifetime. Emme tells us about boys thinking that they are better in science than girls, and she also shows us that bias in action. She tells us about how she grew in her confidence, and we see it when she holds up the trophy. Show and tell.

It has a great backup singer. My analogy of the backup singer refers to any person, living or dead, famous or not, whom you quote or refer to in your essay. Our young author chooses a brilliant one: Madame Curie, one of the most famous scientists in history — and, of course, a woman.

It moves from popular culture to science. It is so much fun to witness that journey this writer takes us on, from a family gathering focusing on football and popular culture to lessons at the end about her knowledge of science.

Its use of language

It reveals the power of two. The number of examples a writer uses has meaning. When a writer uses two examples, they are asking the reader to compare and contrast. In that sense, Emme offers two moments of triumph: the football pool and the science trivia contest. They are alike, but different. The first one leaves her disappointed because the boys reveal a belief that they are or should be better than girls. In the second, she is cheered and celebrated by all.

It climbs up and down the ladder of language. The writer uses two different types of language. Words that make us think, and words that help us see. Words about ideas, and words about things. A phrase about ideas, such as "awareness of gender roles and societal perceptions" is high on the ladder. But words lower on the ladder, such as "marshmallow launchers" and "pineapple-shaped...trophy" are things we can see and hold in our hands.

It makes good use of white space. OK, I fibbed just a little. The essay wasn't perfect. I did make one suggestion to improve it. I thought, in her original version, Emme's paragraphs were a bit too long. There is nothing wrong with good long paragraphs, except for this: They are harder to read than shorter ones. You know that a sentence ends with a period. But you may not have thought that a paragraph ends with a period followed by white space. That white space helps the reader relax. The reader can see the parts better. If a reader sees a 650-word paragraph, they assume that the meaning, like the visual text, is dense and difficult to plod through.

It has a transformative journey.

It reveals how she overcomes obstacles. It turns out that a character's ability to overcome obstacles remains an enduring pattern in storytelling, one that has existed from the earliest examples of Western literature. You may have heard of an ancient epic called the *Odyssey*, in which it takes the hero ten years to find his way home after the Trojan War. Or think of everything that Harry Potter must suffer, including the murder of his parents when he was an infant, before he can overcome the ultimate evil. The famous novelist Kurt Vonnegut advises writers to create a likable character and then spend five hundred pages doing terrible things to him. The idea is to see what the hero is made of. In Emme Slaughter's case, she has 650 words, not 650 pages, but we see what she is made of—in her family and in her education—by overcoming traditional obstacles placed in the path of women's achievement.

It ups the ante. Emme's essay moves in lots of ways. One move is from less serious to more serious. She wins in a fantasy football league. Then she wins at a science camp. Then she chooses Marie Curie, one of history's most famous scientists, as a role model. This is clearly a resilient young woman who would thrive in a demanding academic environment.

It has a strong ending. I think of a good ending as a gold coin the writer gives the reader for making the journey. Thanks for reading all the way through. This reward is for you. What makes Emme's ending so strong is that she has foreshadowed it, beginning with the title and then building steam through the text.

Epilogue: The world of science, from the time Emme was a little girl, imposed obstacle after obstacle to her achieving her dreams.

Paul Cottle, a physics professor at Florida State University, writes about how few women wind up in his engineering, math, and computer science classes. The number can be as low as one in five, even though many universities are more than 60 percent female. That last data point may make it harder for women to get into schools that do not want a great imbalance between women and men.

I caught up with Emme's work at the University of Florida, the college of her choice. As a sophomore, she earned a position as a research assistant to a science professor. She wrote in a text: "Yes, we will be doing biosignature detection using gas chromatography-mass spectrometry with the Mars Rover and other landers!! And then doing field work and running rock samples through the GC-MS system here and comparing them with the samples we get from the Rover data to search for evidence of life beyond Earth!! I start tomorrow 🔥." It appears the young woman, whose boy cousins mocked her in her youth, is living her dream to become an astrophysicist.

So far you have seen the essay by Sam French, which reveals his wit, his charm, and his intelligence. Then you met Emme Slaughter, who shows us her brains, her commitment, and her determination. I did not coach either Sam or Emme, even though I have known their families since they were young children. Both have the advantage of being born into families where reading and writing are very important. Sam is the son of a prize-winning journalist and an outstanding high school English teacher. I have worked with Emme's mom, Holly Slaughter, who is a leader among language arts teachers in the public schools. I think it's cool that neither Sam nor Emme sought out their parents for help when it came time to write their essay. Each wrote the essay that only they could write.

PART II

Grabbing the Reader
by the Throat

From this section you can learn:

* How to decide what should come first in your essay
* The value of placing something cool — or hot! — at the beginning of your story
* What it takes to write a good lead, a first move that hooks the reader and captures the focus of the story
* The writer always has choices — not necessarily good or bad — about ways to influence the reader.

Admissions officers make up a specialized audience for a piece of writing. Buried under hundreds or thousands of applications, an officer has little time, perhaps five minutes or less, to devote to each one. A reader may spend less than thirty seconds reading your essay, perhaps even skip out after ten seconds if you make a bad first impression.

How to avoid that fate? Grab that reader by the throat. Give that reader an opening sentence that sticks. Then make the next part so irresistible that the reader can't look away. Reward that reader for staying with your story.

My nephew Matthew graduated from a college in Scranton, Pennsylvania. I remember when he was in a serious accident. He and his friends were snow tubing down an icy hill when he collided with a tree, injuring his left side. He was rushed to a hospital, where his spleen was removed. He recovered well and has led a healthy life. And the experience gave him the lead in to his college essay:

"The first time I saw your beautiful campus was out the window of an emergency helicopter."

Journalists are famous for grabbing the reader's interest by telling the reader exactly why a story is important right in the opening sentence: "After 40 long years, the people of Libya have freed themselves of a tyrant's rule." Novelists, too, know that a customer in a bookstore may pick up a book, read the first paragraphs, and decide whether to spend that $29.99.

Some literary first lines are so famous that they are easy to remember and quote:

- "Call me Ishmael," a three-word beginning to the six-hundred-page novel *Moby-Dick*, by Herman Melville
- "I am an invisible man," by novelist Ralph Ellison. Many novel titles derive from a phrase that occurs deep into the story. Here in *Invisible Man*, the title appears in the first five words.
- "It was a queer, sultry summer, the summer they electrocuted the Rosenbergs, and I didn't know what I was doing in New York." I remember picking *The Bell Jar* off the shelf at Haslam's Book Store and glancing at that first sentence. I was hooked — and astonished later when author Sylvia Plath echoes that reference to the electric chair in the shock therapy the main character receives after a mental breakdown.

In each of the following examples, drawn from actual student essays, you will find a first draft of an opening sentence, followed by a revision that gives it some juice. For each case, think about why the second version is more likely to grab the reader. Try to come up with a revision that might make it even better.

CASE #1

Before: I'm always trying to overcome my fears. It's hard for me to try something new.

After: I don't know how I got here, but I am nine thousand feet above sea level, looking down from a sharp cliff and wondering whether mountain climbing was a good way to overcome my fear of heights.

CASE #2

Before: I believe that in America tolerance and diversity are very important.

After: I remember the day in homeroom when one student yelled at another for being "unpatriotic" and "un-American." The yeller was wearing her ROTC uniform. The victim wore a headdress, signifying her Muslim faith.

CASE #3

Before: I have been very active in school activities and work hard to be a multitalented person.

After: When people see my blond hair — it's natural! — and hear that I am a cheerleader, they often jump to conclusions about who I am. Then they learn I have published twenty-seven poems and thirteen essays — and suddenly things look a little different.

CASE #4

Before: I have always wanted to attend Calusa College because it had a very good program in social work, and I want to be a social worker someday.

After: My life changed the day that I walked into Serenity Nursing Home as a high school volunteer and had my foot run over by a ninety-three-year-old woman named Bessie Howard.

CASE #5

Before: From the time I was a little girl, I was always interested in reading.

After: In my wallet I keep a torn photograph of a little girl, maybe seven or eight years old. She sits in her backyard near a swing set in a tiny, round pool of water, the plastic kind that your mom or dad had to inflate. You can't see her face, but there are three things that identify her: curly pigtails, a Wonder Woman swimsuit, and the book she is reading. That girl is me.

This next lesson is important: Don't think you have to write one of these snappy leads on your first try. If it doesn't come out like one of these, you may become discouraged. Just write a "before" version of your opening sentence; then, once you know what the story is really about, you can go back and punch up your lead through revision.

HOW TO BEGIN: THE WRITER HAS CHOICES.

It's hard, of course, to judge the true value of the lead sentence or paragraph of a personal essay without reading the entire story. Sometimes an essay will begin too slowly or with an anecdote that in the end is off the mark.

To help you understand the choices you have in writing an essay — including the decision of how to begin it — I am going to introduce you to a brand-new college student, a young woman I have known since she was born. Although she had helped me with a number of reading and writing projects, I did not coach her on her essay. Dear readers, please let me introduce you to Charley Daly.

Hemingway's Cats

By Charley Daly

(490 words)

(Gibbs High School, Class of 2023)

Ernest Hemingway is arguably one of the best writers of American literature. Millions of readers and writers look up to Hemingway for his style and thematics from his short stories to his prize-winning novel *The Old Man and the Sea.* His extraordinary yet tragic life moves others. However, the thing that truly inspires and speaks to me about Hemingway is not the life he lived, nor his celebrated literature, but instead his cats.

In the '40s, a boat captain gifted Hemingway with an all-white polydactyl, six-toed, cat aptly named Snow White. Snow White's polydactyl gene was further carried on by her descendants, with more than half of the cats at Hemingway's Key West home, now a museum, exhibiting the six-toed abnormality. But how can an admirer of Hemingway focus so heavily on his cats? Much like the Hemingway cats, I was born with an extra toe.

On Valentine's Day, 2005, my parents were given quite a shock to witness an irregular addition to their newborn's foot. My parents were unsure if this mutation would hinder my well-being going further. With the doctor's advice, my toe was amputated from my right foot to allow me some normality. This genetic mutation is commonly found, occurring in one of one thousand births amongst the general population. Unfortunately, out of the thousands of people I've met throughout my life, I have yet to find someone else who possesses this unique trait.

Every step I take is another reminder that I am unique. Whenever my right foot turns inwards while I walk, my brain tells me I'm deformed. I'm not saying that being polydactyl is terrible, or that I suffer every day. I simply feel alone. It's hard knowing something so common is seldom found. Yet everyone has that one thing that makes them feel complete, for me that is the

Hemingway cats. When my sister told me about these cats for the first time, it felt like a chain was unlocked from around my heart. These cats, ordinary creatures, shared something so personal to me that no other human being I've met has.

Hemingway once said, "A cat has absolute emotional honesty: human beings, for one reason or another, may hide their feelings, but a cat does not." Hemingway's renowned cats are cherished far after his death in 1961. Whether it be that they are animals, or Hemingway's statement is factual, Snow White's descendants do not mind their extra digits or discriminate against one another; they lead their lives normally as cats.

Polydactyl cats are my favorite companions, in a figurative nature. Although I have yet to meet or own one, my personal connection with these felines is impenetrable. Merely being aware of their existence manifests a form of happiness no person can bring me, a sensation of being seen, being found. I relate to Hemingway, not in his deep metaphors of love and loss, but rather in his deep affection for his cats.

WHAT I LEARNED ABOUT CHARLEY DALY

As I write this, Charley Daly is beginning her college career at the St. Petersburg campus of the University of South Florida.

She was a top student in a public high school with an arts magnet program. For the last eighteen years, Charley has been my next-door neighbor. I remember the day she was born, on a Valentine's Day, and I remember her early surgery.

But I did not know the details until I read this essay. I had never heard the term "polydactyl," and I am embarrassed that I had never heard of Hemingway's cats. Although I had talked with Charley over the years about her reading and writing, I did not coach her on this story. It is a winner as it is, but when I work with writers, I like to play a game I call "What would happen if...?"

As in, "What would happen if you ended the story here?" Or "What would happen if you emphasized this detail more?" Or, in this case, "What would happen if you began your story, not with Hemingway, but with the day you were born?" Imagine an essay with this first sentence: "I was born on Valentine's Day — with eleven toes."

When Charley was sitting down to draft her essay, she had at least three wonderful choices for how to begin: with a famous author, with a colony of cats, or with her extra toe. None of these choices is right or wrong, but each has its own effect on the reader. I would vote for that extra toe. Eeny, meeny, miny, moe, wish I had an extra toe (to write about).

Here are the virtues I see in Charley from her essay. She is intelligent, literary, insightful, curious, self-reflective, humorous, and well educated. Ready to bless a college or university with her presence. She is planning to study clinical psychology.

PART III

~———

Choosing and Using a Prompt

From this section you can learn:

* The most common prompts used by colleges and universities
* How to choose among a variety of prompts
* How to find that special object that has a story hiding within
* What it means to overcome an obstacle, and why this makes for a great story
* How to transform the topic within a prompt into a story that only you can write

THAT THING ABOUT YOU

Whenever teaching a workshop where I ask people to write, I always enjoy writing with and for them. I do like showing off a little, but there are many occasions when I stumble or get stuck. The key is that I want to share and demonstrate my knowledge of the writing process. What would happen, then, if I were the one who had to write an admissions essay? I would need a good prompt: a question meant to spark an idea or revive a memory or experience a story that reveals, in the best way, your character.

Somewhere in my travels, I ran into a writing prompt that is a good way to spark a personal essay: "The thing about me is...." It can lead to opening sentences such as these:

- The thing about me is that I only wear purple.
- The thing about me is that I watched the first *Star Wars* movie more than one hundred times.
- The thing about me is I never pay for parking.
- The thing about me is I've never met my biological mother.
- The thing about me is that the first time I played golf, I made a hole in one. My score for the round was 135.

At a writing workshop for professional journalists, I offered this prompt and was delighted to receive an interesting array of responses, each one revealing something personal, quirky, and interesting about the writer. It was a woman who wrote: "The thing about me is I only wear purple." When she read that aloud, I could not believe that it was true. But I did a visual inventory of Ms. Purple, and her blouse, her skirt, her shoes were all shades of purple. I noticed that the face of her watch had a purple design. I was a little embarrassed when she reached under her blouse at the shoulder and inched out a bra strap. It was purple. Whether it's your obsession with the color, a rare genetic mutation, or anything else, the goal is to highlight a quality that is unique to YOU.

As I mentioned, when I give students of any age a prompt, I always like to write with them. It enables me to learn as they are learning, figuring out again how to solve certain writing problems, and, in the end, to share my process with them. Here, then, is what I wrote in a workshop about writing the admissions essay.

The Thing About Me Is...
By Roy Peter Clark

The thing about me is that I like to play the crane, you know that cheesy arcade game you find in malls, movie theaters, and seaside restaurants. The prize is a stuffed toy—a pink giraffe with a blue nose, manufactured in China, of course, at a cost of fractions of pennies per unit. So why am I willing to spend five dollars on "Jeff" — my name for the pink giraffe — whose true value is less than a penny?

First, a disclaimer. I don't gamble at the casinos or racetracks. I don't waste money on cigarettes or booze. And I never spend more than five dollars per crane session.

My wife thinks I'm a fool — "pissing away your money" she calls it — on a rigged game. But she underestimates my expertise. I can look into a crane, study how the toys are stacked, and assess my chances. Vertically stacked with just heads sticking up, the prizes are almost impossible to extract. On their sides, however, they are vulnerable to the coordination of my eyes and a steady right hand.

So why do I do it? The thrill of the hunt? The embarrassment of my bride and three daughters? The occasional smattering of applause from onlookers? The smile on a little kid's face when I hand over one of the prizes? All of those, plus this: I really enjoy accomplishing things others cannot do, or think I cannot do, or consider impossible.

Sure, there are days when I return to the table empty-handed, when my wife might roll her eyes with contempt. But then there was that glorious day when I returned to the table with not one, or two, but three fluffy creatures, including a purple hippo I named Shirley, after my mom.

And then there was that one epic day — in the

bowels of a Tampa mall that no longer exists — when because of a sloppy tangle of tags and strings in the toy pit, I pulled in seven on one try, which must be a world record. How many other students applying to your school can claim a world record?

So, if you happen to have cranes on your college campus that you use as an important source of revenue, you do NOT want to accept me to your school since I'll beat you at your own game. If you want someone who can solve problems, understand spatial reasoning, and is willing to take a chance, I'm your pink giraffe. Snatch me before someone else does.

For the record, that little essay is 416 words. It's OK to like your own writing, and, as I revisited this work, I noticed things that stick out. I like the pink giraffe and the purple hippo, and I really like that they both have names. Giving the name of the dog, or the cat, or your pet snake, or your fluffy pet is that tiny detail that often charms the reader. I also like the way the writer (hey, that's me!) realizes that folks will think of his habit as trivial and wasteful but that he perseveres nonetheless. I enjoyed writing — and experiencing — that scene where I capture seven toys in one shot. Good stories have a payoff, and that feels like one to me.

Readers are attracted, I think, to surprises, especially ones that might make them laugh. Inviting them NOT to accept me, feels like one of those.

So, young readers, what do you think? Would you accept

me into your school? Now sit down and start writing: "The thing about me is...."

SELECTING THE BEST WRITING PROMPT FOR YOU

Using prompts to spark writing is not just a trick used in student writing. Professional writers have their own prompts: an assignment from an editor is a prompt. A news event is a prompt. Your curiosity often prompts you to write. (This book was prompted by a suggestion from an editor!)

But a prompt is not a story. Neither is a topic. "We should write about student absenteeism in the public schools," says an editor to a writer, to which I might respond, "What about it?" Well, it's a prompt, and as a responsible writer who wants to help my editor, it's my job to go out, find things out, check things out, and report things out to the general public.

Some colleges and universities have their own prompts and applications. But there is a handy resource called the Common App, which allows students to use one form to apply to multiple colleges. Over time, the Common App has developed a set of effective writing prompts. As I was writing this book in 2023–24, Meredith Lombardi, director of education and training for the organization that offers the Common App, announced that the prompts would remain the same as the year before.

Feedback from all the stakeholders — students, teachers, counselors, tutors, and others — indicate a high level of

satisfaction with these prompts. The reason they are published early is not to rush you into writing, but to give you
lots of time to explore them and find the one that will lead
you to the story only you can write.

Here is a list of essay prompts for 2023–24, with my reflections below each one.

1. Some students have a background, identity, interest, or
   talent that is so meaningful they believe their application
   would be incomplete without it. If this sounds like you,
   then please share your story.

   This is a version of the "The thing about me is…" prompt,
meant to get you writing about what makes you unique.

2. The lessons we take from obstacles we encounter can be
   fundamental to later success. Recount a time when you
   faced a challenge, setback, or failure. How did it affect
   you, and what did you learn from the experience?

   Emme Slaughter had the perfect take on this prompt,
revealing the male prejudice against her dreams of becoming
a scientist.

3. Reflect on a time when you questioned or challenged a
   belief or idea. What prompted your thinking? What was
   the outcome?

Isn't this prompt the essential mission of adolescence, to challenge ideas and beliefs? It is embodied in popular narratives such as the television series *Young Sheldon*, about a precocious child scientist who declares to his Southern Baptist family that he is an atheist. It turns out to be hilarious, and, at the same time, the source of wonderful explorations of the role of organized religion in American life.

4. Reflect on something that someone has done for you that has made you happy or thankful in a surprising way. How has this gratitude affected or motivated you?

It seems as if using the first person — *I* or *me* — is necessary in an effective personal essay. But sometimes you need, not the *I* but the *eye*. Think of your eye as a magic camera. You can point it at another person or use it to capture a moment in time — when your character was formed or re-formed, or a chance encounter that altered the trajectory of your life. Years ago, a rabbi, a stranger, gave me a book on a train ride from New York to Philadelphia. It changed my view of the world. Decades later, I tracked him down and wrote the story.

5. Discuss an accomplishment, event, or realization that sparked a period of personal growth and a new understanding of yourself or others.

Examples abound of students writing about things they have accomplished. While writing about your achievements gets an admissions officer's attention and reveals your readiness for college life, this is most effective when achievements are coupled with values. I have three accomplished daughters. I would often brag about their achievements: Alison won an award, Emily got a promotion, Lauren was cast in a musical. More impressive, however, would be to tell a story about how Alison is a person of great empathy, how Emily has worked hard and saved money since she was 15, and how Lauren tutors aspiring college students in mathematics.

6. Describe a topic, idea, or concept you find so engaging that it makes you lose all track of time. Why does it captivate you? What or who do you turn to when you want to learn more?

This prompt is so cool. It describes a universal experience to which we never pay enough attention. Some scholars talk about the power of "flow," of being so immersed in an experience that we lose all track of time. Reading and writing can do this for me. So can a wonderful movie, or a phone conversation with an old friend.

7. Share an essay on any topic of your choice. It can be one you've already written, one that responds to a different prompt, or one of your own design.

I hope the examples in this book will spark many ideas. Go for it.

* * *

In her research on which colleges to apply to, a young friend, Stacey Lim, compiled a list of two types of essays. The first can be found in the core application essays, like the ones that appear on the previous pages. But some colleges and universities offer prompts that are specific to their school. Among those she researched:

Duke University: "Tell us about an intellectual experience in the past two years that you found absolutely fascinating."

Davidson College: "We encourage students to explore curiosities in and out of the classroom. What is a topic, activity, or idea that excites you? Tell us why. Examples may include hobbies, books, interactions, music, podcasts, movies, etc. (250–300 word limit)"

Wake Forest University: "Dr. Maya Angelou, renowned author, poet, civil-rights activist, and former Wake Forest University Reynolds Professor of American Studies, inspired others to celebrate their identities and to honor each person's dignity. Choose one of Dr. Angelou's powerful quotes. How does this quote relate to your lived experience or reflect how you plan to contribute to the Wake Forest community? (limit 300 words)"

Georgia Tech: "Why do you want to study your chosen major specifically at Georgia Tech? (max 300 words)"

Choosing a prompt might seem overwhelming at first. But it doesn't have to be. Just sit down with a pencil and a yellow pad. Do not censor yourself or reject an idea too early. Try to come up with ten ideas for responding to each prompt. If you can't think of that many, call in your helpers to brainstorm with you. What is normal to you may seem extraordinary to them.

As I typed each of these additional essay prompts, I immediately began to imagine a story from my life that would satisfy the requirement. As I rehearsed these, I realized that I was calling upon all the strategies I describe in this book. I doubt you will be presented with a writing challenge you cannot meet with these writing strategies.

Part IV

Steps of the Writing Process

From this section you can learn:

* Good writing is not magic but the result of a process, a set of steps.
* Focus is central to the process.
* There are things you can do when you get stuck.
* Rehearsal is the antidote to procrastination.

A PICTURE OF THE WRITING PROCESS

I have written this book in the hope that your admissions essay will not be the only thing you ever write. The larger vision imagines you as a highly literate person, someone who reads with insight, who writes for a variety of audiences, and who can talk about how reading and writing create meaning for all the players. The questions and suggestions in this book will invite you to engage in those "literate behaviors," actions that will build muscles that make you a stronger student, a more productive and satisfied professional, and even a better citizen.

When you read a good essay, you may think that it takes some magic skill to create it, a power that you lack. But good writing is not magic. The great writing teacher Donald Murray taught me that writing is a rational process, a series of steps that you can practice and learn. He believed, and I, too, believe, that all writers across generations and genres face the same basic problems. Whether you are writing a sonnet, a screenplay, a report, or an essay, the writer will look for solutions to the same challenges:

What will I write about?
What information do I need to gather?
How can I find a focus?
How can I select the best stuff?
What comes first?
How can I get my hands moving?
What parts of the work should I make better?

As a shorthand, you can remember the parts of the process with these seven words:

Idea

Collect

Focus

Select

Order

Draft

Revise

Let's explore each step in more detail, with reference to the personal essay.

THE IDEA STAGE

Unless you get a specific assignment or prompt, you may suffer from the misapprehension that you have nothing to write about. I was that way, too, especially as a young writer. If you had asked me to write a personal essay while I was in high school, I would have made a mental list of possible topics, and crossed out each one as boring or uninteresting. Now I can look back upon those years and think of countless topics, probably enough for a full autobiography or memoir.

"What was it like to be in a first-grade class with sixty-five other students and one teacher, Sister Mary Leone?"

"Sitting in the top of a tall sycamore tree reading a

book about vampires, an adult work that my parents did not want me to read."

"Making my first dollar shoveling snow after a huge blizzard."

My transformation as a writer is from having no writing ideas to now seeing the world as a storehouse of story ideas.

Fortunately, college applications usually include one or more prompts. I've already shared one of my favorites, "The thing about me is...." Here are a few others:

"You own an object—a photo, a book, a gift, an heirloom—that has an important story hiding inside it. Write about that object and why it has meaning for you."

"In school, we learn not just from books or lessons or lectures. We learn from our experiences with others. Think of a day in high school when something happened that made you realize something important about you or the world."

"Lost and found. We all lose things and find them again, or not. Or we find things that others have lost. Write about such a time, what happened, and what you learned from the experience."

We'll explore in more depth how to respond to prompts. The key is to see them as open doors, not locked ones, designed to generate ideas, not limit them.

THE COLLECT STAGE

You may be wondering how much collecting, reporting, or researching you might have to do for an essay that may be no longer than three hundred words. The answer is "More than you think."

I have learned so much by working with the youngest writers, and also the oldest. I taught Gillian Gaynair when she was ten years old, a fifth grader at Bay Point Elementary School in St. Petersburg, Florida. Some of the stories she wrote back then made their way into my first book *Free to Write: A Journalist Teaches Young Writers*. She is now fifty-three years old and has enjoyed a long and productive writing career at newspapers and nonprofits.

In high school, if she interviewed the new principal of a school and profiled that person, she would use most of the details she had collected in her notebook.

This is a common pattern for writers of every age. When you gather a lot of stuff, some of it will be more interesting and important, some of it less. Having it available in your notes or files or early drafts gives you the opportunity to put your BEST stuff in your essay — the coolest little story, the most amazing thing that someone said, the number that jumps off the page.

But what kind of content do you collect for a personal essay?

1. **Your memories of people and experiences**: I jog my memory by sitting at the computer, or with my phone, or

on a yellow pad and begin writing down scenes that have stuck in my mind, or people I have met, or places that were important to me, and more.

2. **Old photos (or new ones):** I have one photo of myself as a boy reading a book. In the image, I am laughing. Just looking at that photo transports me to another place and time. Old photos or movies or videos are time machines. You can see yourself at a moment in time, a powerful spark for writing. Now, of course, you carry your camera — the one on your phone — in your pocket. If you are writing about the dog you rescued from the park, you can capture visual images of the place where it happened — and revisit it later, to jog your memory.

3. **Documents like albums or yearbooks:** I am lucky because my parents took lots of photos of me growing up and placed them in albums, which I still have. I have my eighth-grade autograph book from 1962, and, even better, my mother's high school autograph book from 1937, which contains pressed flowers she wore at a dance. My mother kept a satin-covered baby book that describes my earliest adventures. I have all my high school and college yearbooks. These are treasure troves of memories.

4. **Conversations with family members:** Do you remember the day you were born? Of course not. But someone does: a parent, grandparent, siblings, other relatives and neighbors. My first trip out of the hospital in March of 1948 was in a taxicab with Mom and Dad, driving from a Jewish hospital in Brooklyn across the Brooklyn Bridge to a

one-bedroom apartment on the Lower East Side of Manhattan, known as Knickerbocker Village. I know about this because people told me.

5. **Interviews with people in the know**: Maybe your passion is the electric guitar, or bowling, or saving brown pelicans from fishing lines. Whatever it is, there are people out there who share your passion — some, perhaps, who have taken it to places you have yet to imagine. Conversations with them can make your brainstorming even brainier and stormier.

6. **Search engines**: A great benefit of a cell phone is having an encyclopedia in your pocket. By now we know that if we have forgotten who starred in that movie or want to know who is singing that song we hear in the coffee shop, the answer is at our fingertips. When I was in high school, encyclopedias came in sets — maybe twenty or more thick volumes, each one heavy enough to serve as a doorstop. Now we have Wikipedia. It's a great resource — but not always a reliable one, so if you use it to help you describe an author or film director who has influenced your view of the world, it's always good to double-check.

7. **Books and movies**: I think, I hope, it's fair to say that college admissions officers like potential students who read books. Reading a book may help you develop a particular idea, such as how growing trees may help save the planet. And allusions to various authors (J.R.R. Tolkien, James Baldwin, Flannery O'Connor, Elie Wiesel) or culturally relevant movies may be windows into your intelligence, curiosity, and spirit.

I remember coaching Molly Jacobson, the daughter of a friend, when she wrote a charming and tricky essay on the way her body changed dramatically in the summer before eighth grade. I've read lots of good essays over the years on this topic, including from great authors such as Nora Ephron.

In our conversation, I introduced Molly to the literature of metamorphosis — of dramatic change, from the legends of Greek mythology to the fiction of Franz Kafka, who turns his human character into a giant insect. Comparing her real-life experience of how boys and girls began to notice her and treat her differently to relevant stories from literature made Molly seem both brainy and funny. She had a fine college experience at Barnard.

THE FOCUS STAGE

Every piece of writing needs a clear focus, or what we sometimes call a "theme," "thesis," or "central idea." To get to the focus, writers ask themselves the question: "What is this about?" Or, better yet, "What is it REALLY about?"

If I try to describe the focus of a novel, such as *The Grapes of Wrath*, or a significant work of nonfiction, such as *Hiroshima*, I might venture to say that *The Grapes of Wrath* is about how Depression-era poverty and joblessness were made worse by corporate greed and malicious police power. In *Hiroshima*, the focus is on the effects that the dropping of the atomic bomb by American forces had upon civilian survivors, through eyewitness testimony.

Your focus, for a 500-word essay, won't be that broad or grand, of course. In fact, the narrower the focus, the better. You want to convey it in just a sentence or two. As you think about a focus for a college admissions essay, you might be tempted to say that the focus is to make this point: "I am a smart, curious, productive, interesting person who will make your school a better place, so please accept me." But that's the Big Telling. Your true focus will best be conveyed by the Small Showing.

A strong focus will help you figure out how to begin, which examples to include, and how to organize all the elements into a coherent whole.

Here is how I could describe the focus of each of the sample essays you have read so far:

Sam French: I am willing to take good risks — in my life and in my writing.

Emme Slaughter: I will compete against men any day on the way to becoming a scientist. Get used to it.

Roy Peter Clark: I love to compete — in big things and in small. Accept me and meet your eventual salutatorian.

THE SELECT STAGE

Let's review the process steps so far. We begin with an idea for a story or essay. We hunt and gather, from our memory and other sources, elements to include. As we collect, what might start as a wide topic or vague idea begins to come into a sharper focus. If we have done the work, and if we are a little lucky, that focus may give us a title, and maybe a first sentence or paragraph — what journalists like to call a lead.

But as you look at your notes, you may find yourself stuck: "I just can't figure out which parts to include and which parts to leave out." That indecision may be a sign that your focus isn't sharp enough. To use two different metaphors: a good focus, expressed in a good lead, is a kind of door that invites the relevant elements in. Or it's a kind of knife that cuts the irrelevant parts out.

These questions will help you select your best material:

> Which of these is most important, interesting, or memorable?
> Which ones support the main idea that I want to lead with?
> Which ones would be good for the beginning, middle, or end?

When I have a list of possible elements in my notes, I learn a lot from reading them with a pen in my hand. I have an easy system of annotation. If I know I will not use a quote or an anecdote, I just place a big *X* in the margin. If I don't know yet whether I will use something or if I'm not sure of its meaning or value, I use a question mark. If something is good, I put a star in the margin: *. If it is really good or great, I put two stars * *, or three * * *.

Finally, I look at my notes and begin to imagine the structure of the story, so I may see a quote or an anecdote or a memory and mark it with a comment such as "Might make a good ending."

One of my books is titled *Murder Your Darlings*, a bit of writing advice that goes back a century. The title refers to what writers should do with elements in a story that may be clever but fail to sharpen the point of the work. But you don't have to kill your favorites; you can just save them for another essay.

The personal essay, and the process of writing in general, is an act of curation. And often, this means making the tough choices about which darlings will be murdered, and which will live to fight another day. For example, the first draft of a commencement speech I delivered had eight anecdotes about my mom. (The event was near Mother's Day, and I knew there would be lots of happy moms in the audience.) But by the time I wrote a final version, those eight became five became three became one became none. I realized that while those stories were entertaining, they did not support my main theme: that life has a way of getting you to the place you need to be, not to the place you wanted to be.

Even better, I now had ample material for a spectacular Mother's Day story.

THE ORDER STAGE

The first edition of my most popular writing book, *Writing Tools*, has fifty chapters. The cool thing about chapters is that you can write them one at a time, and you don't have to choose a final order until late in the process. I favor short chapters for my books, about one thousand words, but that may be twice as long as your personal essay.

Chapters are just one way of organizing a written work. The *Oxford English Dictionary* has twelve volumes, and a Japanese-style haiku has three lines:

The mockingbird dives
At the cat crouched in high grass
To protect its nest

That poem (I just wrote it looking out at our oak tree) follows a rigid predetermined structure. Just as a sonnet is a poem with fourteen lines, the haiku has three lines (comprising seventeen syllables). You can count them. The first line has five syllables (I counted them on my fingers), the second line has seven, and the third has five.

My point is that every meaningful text has a beginning, a middle, and an end. You may have a great idea and a sharp focus; you may have collected lots of stuff and selected the best; but you still have to create an order. The best work has recognizable parts, elements that fit together nicely to create a pleasing whole. And when the big parts fit together in a sequence that makes sense, we call that good feeling coherence.

Even a short essay has a beginning, a lead or introduction that compels the reader to learn more. The middle provides the evidence, if you will, supporting the lead with good examples, anecdotes, or ideas. The ending can be a perfect summary or conclusion, or may surprise the reader with a startling insight. You create the vehicle that takes the reader on a journey.

THE DRAFT STAGE

This is a good time to give you permission, not that you need it, to skip over everything I've written so far, and jump right to the drafting stage. That means you just sit down (or you can do it standing up!) and write, say, five hundred words from your brain — without any collecting, focusing, selecting, or ordering.

I do this now and then when I am writing a personal column for the *Tampa Bay Times*. I might just sit and start typing about something that happened to me: "Our house alarm went off at 4 o'clock this morning, and I jumped out of bed like the Flash, looking for fires or burglars. It turned out that the system needed a new battery."

I am not calling this a first draft. In a way, it's something more helpful. Call it a zero draft. Too many writers suffer because they wait too long to begin turning thoughts into language. A zero draft teaches me what I already know and what I need to learn.

There are two great obstacles faced by writers when they begin writing. One is procrastination; the other is writer's block. The antidote to procrastination is something we call rehearsal. If you have ever asked someone out on a date or asked a boss for a raise, you know how to rehearse.

I have drafted many a story in my head, on a rare occasion in my dreams. So, as you work on your personal essay, feel free to imagine it. How could I start or end it? What will be the most interesting thing, and where will I put it? That is how I composed an 1,800-word commencement address. I spent more than two months writing it in my head: as I walked around the park, unpacked the dishwasher, took a shower, stared at the ceiling in bed. When I finally got my butt in the chair and my hands moving, I wrote an eight-thousand-word zero draft in almost no time: all that rehearsing built up in the anticipation of release.

Writer's block is a little different. Your butt is already in the chair, your hands are on the keyboard, but nothing is coming out. It is not easy to do, but the most effective explosive to break through that block is — get ready for this — to lower your standards. Just remember that no one cares whether your zero draft is any good, because no one will ever see it. The admissions officers will judge you by what turns out to be your third draft, or your eleventh draft, or whatever it takes to get to a final product you are happy with.

Some drafting advice that works for me:

- Start early. This is good advice for any writer writing about any topic at any time. Writers, even great ones, have the reputation of waiting for as long as they can to begin drafting, depending upon adrenaline and deadlines to push them over the finish line. Remember that you can be rehearsing your essay in your head for weeks, even months before you slide your butt into the chair and get your hands moving. The earlier you start, the more opportunity you will leave for coaching and revision. If you are in the second semester of your junior year, it makes sense to start thinking about your essay topic. You have plenty of time to change your mind.
- Write or type quickly. Don't stop too often to correct spellings or other mistakes — that can wait till later.
- If you have notes, put them aside. Let your fingers draw from your mind what you already know.
- Write more than you need. You'll get from one thousand words to three hundred words (or whatever your target is) through revision — the final stage of the process.
- Tell that negative voice to shut up while you get some work done.

THE REVISION STAGE

My favorite part of the writing process is revision. You have already done the hardest work, and now you have an opportunity to "see it again." That is what re-vision literally means.

Too many people act as if revision is the same as proofreading. It isn't. Proofreading is when we check over a text in search of inaccuracies, needless repetitions, and mistakes in spelling, grammar, or syntax. Revision is much more interesting and complicated, because it can apply to any part of the process. You can revise the idea, or the collection of details, or the focus. You can select different scenes, reorganize the parts, and, of course, change all elements of the draft.

If you aren't sure what elements of your essay need revising, try reading your work out loud. When I am working on a personal essay, I often call my daughter Alison in Atlanta and read an early draft over the phone. She likes her dad's work, and that builds my confidence. But it also gives me a chance to notice the parts that make her laugh or the points where she seems confused, and to ask her questions such as "Did that ending work for you?"

But here is an important secret: Every time I read something aloud, I find something I want to change, either because it lacks a good rhythm, or because I don't like the way it makes me sound, perhaps too glib, or angry, or show-offy. On those occasions when I have recorded the audio version of one of my books, I have revised sentences because I had trouble reading them aloud. I did not see any problems with my eyes, but I heard them with my ears.

You can even revise a revision: multiple times, in fact. I know a writer who decided to switch the beginning with the ending, and then switch them back. I know another writer who took all the commas out and then put them all back in. Some writers revise so much that editors have to encourage — or even force — them to turn in their work.

So when do you know when you're done revising? Often, a writer will stop revising only when they have to meet a deadline. One trick I learned to get around this was the artificial deadline. If my editor wants the story by Friday, I fool myself into thinking the deadline is Wednesday. That forces me to write drafts earlier than I think I can. That leaves me time for revision. It also means I will deliver the work on time, giving the editors time they need to do their best work.

It is important for you to know that when I write a book such as this one, I have a tremendous amount of help. My agent guides me, and, of course, my editor. My editor usually gets her assistant to read the text and make suggestions. Then the manuscript is turned over to a master copy editor, who marks it up with fact-checking, suggested deletions, and various other improvements.

I am telling you this so you know it is OK for you to get help on your personal essay. If I benefit from it, so should you — as long as you do it ethically and honestly.

PART V

Craft of Honest Writing

From this section you can learn:

* Tools of originality to help you avoid the unethical borrowing of other people's work
* Strategies of writing and research that help you overcome the temptation to make things up
* The most helpful and most honest way to deal with writing chatbots and other digital tools
* Creating and presenting the most authentic version of yourself

A GOOD WRITER IS AN HONEST WRITER

You not only want to be a good writer; you also want to be an honest one. In fact, I would argue that the only good writers are the honest ones.

There are two great sins in writing, and they can get you into trouble. The first is one that you have likely been warned about at other points in your academic life: plagiarism. That's when you use someone's work and claim it as your own. If you were to copy one of the good student essays in this book (or any other book, or the internet) and send it with your application to Princeton, that would be plagiarism.

There are other ways to cheat your way in. You can buy an essay online. Or you could pay someone you know to write one. Don't. Each of these shortcuts is almost certain to backfire. Even if it helps get you in, which is doubtful, it would leave a shadow that could follow you for the rest of your career.

The other sin is fabrication. That is when a writer invents a scene or a conversation that never happened. If you label the piece of writing fiction, that's OK, but college admissions officers are not looking for works of fiction; they are looking for the truth about you.

I could write about the day I jumped off a fishing boat into the Gulf of Mexico and saved a child from drowning. You might think well of me — until I confess that it never happened and that, in truth, I can barely swim. More important, if you make up a story and include it in your college essay, the reader won't get to know the real you. As someone who has read countless student essays, I can attest that my Spider-sense begins to tingle at a mere whiff of inauthenticity. That's even more true of admissions officers, who have seen — and read — it all.

Now along comes a paradigm-shifting technology called artificial intelligence. AI is evolving and mutating so quickly that it makes little sense to describe its current state here. For our purposes, think of AI as a quick-thinking, quick-writing robot. Using it as a research tool is honest. Using it to write your essay for you is not.

Let say your essay includes information about the year you were born. In my case, that would be 1948. I might ask a chatbot like ChatGPT or Google's Gemini to list the most significant events that happened in the world that year. Almost before I could take another breath, I would have a list or a few paragraphs that answer my question. I could use those answers, for example, in an essay about how early television sets were being sold by the millions that year, and how my first dream was to grow up to be a cowboy, like the ones my dad and I watched on TV. Or how I got a Hopalong Cassidy outfit — hat, holster, little six-shooters — for my fourth birthday.

But remember this: The answers from AI may be wrong, so you should make sure to verify them using another trusted source. And when you sit down to write your essay, don't forget that it remains out of bounds to include actual text generated by the bot.

Here is another problem. The chatbot did not invent the text it delivered to you. It is not a creator, as we understand that word. It is a hunter and gatherer, one that can work with incredible speed. So where does that information and that language come from? We just cannot tell — at least not yet.

That means if you use a significant amount of language — say a paragraph — from an AI answer, you are not just making unfair use of a machine, you are not giving credit to the author or authors who wrote the language processed by the bot. Think of it as an act of double-decker stealing.

But here's what you can do: Use technology for research, let the reader know your sources, follow accepted guidelines for fair use, and paraphrase or summarize sources in your own words.

Think of the college essay as the story that only you can write. Perhaps more than anything you ever write, it will stand for you, represent you, speak for you, promote you, elevate you in the eyes of readers. That can happen only if it is written with your words, in your own voice.

Practice those behaviors now, and you are on your way to becoming a good and honest writer.

RED LIGHT, GREEN LIGHT

So far, I have listed only the Red Light ethics: Don't do this, don't do that — or else.

In the long run, the Green Light ethics count for more.

Green Light ethics refer to what you can do; even what you *should* do.

- Learn and practice the tools of originality and voice, including many listed in this book.
- If you have access to responsible coaching, use it. Of course I would say that: I am a writing coach! I have helped many students with their essays. But it is not my job to tell students what to write about, and certainly not to write their essays for them. Instead, I may read a draft and offer feedback. Or I may ask them questions at different parts of the process. For example, I recently coached a student who is a champion sailor. I said to her, "You have written about how scary sailing can be. Can you tell me about a specific time when you were scared?" Rosie told me about the time a sudden Florida squall tipped her boat on its end so she was looking straight down. She now plans to include it in her essay. Even if you don't have access to formal coaching, it is OK to seek support, feedback, or proofreading from a coach, teacher, editor, relative, even other students who have your confidence.

PART VI

Writing with Your Authentic Voice

From this section you can learn:

* What we mean when we talk about a writer's "voice"
* Strategies to help you modulate your voice and influence the reader's experience
* How to write so you sound like yourself — or a little better
* The value of reading your work aloud
* How to read your own work and others' with your eyes and ears

WHAT DO WE MEAN BY THE WRITER'S VOICE?

The word *voice* is often used by writers and readers to describe that feeling that the writer is speaking to the reader or listener. Sometimes, a writer reads their work aloud — as in a podcast or a public radio report. Through their literal voice, they are able to showcase their unique style or personality to the audience. But an admissions officer will be reading your text without hearing your speaking voice. So in order for your unique personality and flair to shine through, there are things you can do to create the illusion that you are speaking.

Write the way you speak is common advice, but even better advice is to write *at least a little better* than you speak. When you go in for a job interview, you usually try to look better than usual. You are not wearing a costume, but you are trying to make a good first impression. The same is true with your writing.

I have the advantage of being a musician. Since the Beatles arrived in America in 1964 (when I was a high school sophomore) I have played in a rock band. I could write a great personal essay about those experiences with the Henchmen, T.S. and the Eliots, Tuesday's Children, the Sidewinders, the Fabulous Nosecaps, the St. Pete Florida Blues Band, and countless side gigs.

Think for a minute of all the common language used to describe music and writing. Both are called compositions. Both use notes. Both can have rhythm, repetitions, slow and fast parts, intros, transitions, crescendos, and codas or conclusions. Songs tell stories, with discrete parts that move and fit together. Both have voice.

I am no expert on sound. But I have watched sound engineers use mixing boards, adjusting sounds with different levers: more or less volume, more or less bass or treble, a little reverb here, and so on.

As a writer, you have those same levers available to you, too. They work great in a personal essay. Some have technical names, but I will present them in the simplest way possible:

PRONOUN POWER

One way to tune your voice is to make a purposeful decision about whether to use *I*, *you*, or *they*.

You may have heard that pronouns have "person."

The first-person singular is *I* or *me*. The plural is *we* or *us*.

The second-person singular and plural is *you*.

The third-person singular is *he/him, she/her, it*. To avoid mischaracterizations and gender issues, many people, including me, use the singular *they/them*. That is also the plural form.

Your writing voice will change depending upon which

person you choose to use. In general, the first-person singular points the camera at you, either to express your opinion or to show yourself as a character in a story or anecdote. You become the narrator.

The first-person plural — as in "We the people" — is a tool writers use to reveal their identity or to show themselves as part of a group. (I might use it to describe all of us high school boys who wanted to be in bands after we witnessed the popularity of the Beatles.)

The second-person singular or plural creates the illusion of conversation, as if you were sitting across from someone in a coffee shop. Addressing the reader directly works for me when I am sharing something I think is especially valuable for them to know about me. The second-person plural — meaning "all of you" or "some of you" — comes in super-handy when you are delivering a commencement speech in front of twelve thousand people.

If the first person is most personal and the second person is most conversational, then it is fair to call the third person the most neutral or objective. That is why so many informational reports are delivered in the third person. I don't want to hear about what the writer is feeling; I don't want to engage in a discourse with an imagined reader; I want to report that Hurricane Idalia is within hours of landfall and there is still time to evacuate low-lying areas.

Of course, you can, carefully, switch from one person to another, from the *I* to the *you*, but read that shift aloud to hear if it sounds right.

LEVEL OF LANGUAGE

All of us use language that is high or low or somewhere in the middle. It can be very effective in a personal essay to move up and down in your language, depending upon what you are trying to say. Remember if your language is just high, you may sound scholarly, philosophical, intellectual, which may be good for someone trying to enter an elite college, but it can also mask your full personality. If your language is consistently low, to the level of slang, you may come across as unready for college-level studies.

My mom bought me a thesaurus when I was a sixth grader. Always looking to impress, I wrote sentences that had words like "incarcerate," rather than "jail," "prevaricate," rather than "lie," or "expectorate," rather than "spit." I made myself sound like a snooty intellectual, like the TV child scientist on *Young Sheldon*. The goal in good writing is not to use the biggest word, but the *best* one.

I had the honor of visiting South Africa during its first democratic elections in 1994. I could write that it was thrilling to watch the dawn of a new democracy. That language is pretty high, evoking the lofty concept of democracy being born. But what does democracy look like? To help the reader experience it, I might describe how amazing it was to see lines of thousands of Black South Africans winding for miles and miles toward the polls or how it took two strong men to carry their ninety-year-old grandmother to the voting booth for the first time in her life. That language is a little more accessible. I have climbed down the ladder to something we can see and feel.

We will see many examples of good personal essays in which the writers move up to express meaning, and down to show you real life in action.

CHOOSING YOUR BACKUP SINGERS

Writers are often judged by whom they quote or to whom they allude. The best public speakers know how to do this well. A fancier way to describe this is to make purposeful decisions about your range of allusions. Your voice is your own, but the best vocalists have backup singers. Even the great Gladys Knight had her Pips.

I just made an allusion to a great soul singer. I could have chosen many others, but she is so classy and soulful. That reference shows that I have impeccable taste in music; that I understand why this iconic singer is often referred to as the Empress of Soul. It also probably identifies me as a baby boomer whose musical tastes developed in the 1950s and '60s.

Your backup singers will reflect your generation, your cultural preferences, and the names that have special meaning to you. My Dusty Springfield might be your Taylor Swift. My Ella Fitzgerald might be your Beyoncé.

You will notice that I chose a reference to popular culture, but I can go high culture, too, if it suits my purpose. I could mention that almost two thousand years ago a Roman poet and teacher named Horace wrote that the highest purpose of all literature is to "delight and instruct." By demonstrating a surprising range of backup singers, I can reveal myself in ways that reaffirm who I am and that I hope will impress others.

LENGTH AND COMPLEXITY OF YOUR SENTENCES

It's not a rule, just a matter of style, that stories "sound" better if the writer varies the length and structure of sentences. A sequence of sentences the same length runs the risk of sounding boring.

I have a secret vice. I love to play the crane. It costs fifty cents per try. I almost never win. It just doesn't matter. If I see a crane, I play the crane.

There is nothing grammatically wrong with those sentences. They are true and reveal something fun, I hope, about my personality. But when I read them aloud, they sound robotic. On the other hand, a series of long sentences can tire out readers, who, if they are like me, want to come up for air.

I don't think much about sentence length when I am drafting a story, but during revision, I notice opportunities. Long sentences can help you build an inventory. You can write: "I remember the first pack of baseball cards I purchased with my own money. When I opened it, a slab of pink bubble gum rested upon a deck that included Yogi Berra, Al Kaline, Jackie Robinson, Roberto Clemente, and Whitey Ford, all who wound up in the Baseball Hall of Fame. Best dime I ever spent."

See what I just did? I began with a sentence of medium length, followed with a longer inventory, and then dropped the mic with a sentence of only five words. A short sentence is one great way to end a paragraph. The short sentence lends a kind of credibility to the text and signals that you really believe what you are saying. It's a way to deliver the gospel truth.

EXAMPLES OF ESSAYS WITH VOICE

It was as early as 2012 that the Poynter Institute, the school where I teach writing, decided to offer classes for students preparing to write their college essays. My partner in this effort was Kelly McBride, who currently serves as the public editor of National Public Radio. It was her idea to harvest some examples of short personal essays as they were broadcast on Youth Radio (now YR Media), an excellent format for young writers who want to tune their voices both on the page and over the air. These next two essays from back then were developed as radio scripts, not as admissions essays. But they serve as excellent examples of what it looks like and sounds like when young writers find their authentic voices.

Return of the Girly Girl

By Sasha Black

(399 words)

I sometimes wear a pink tiara. And not just in the privacy of my home. I've worn it roaming the halls of my school or even the streets of Atlanta. People probably wouldn't notice if I were five. But I'm a few months shy of eighteen, and I'm constantly asked about my choice of headgear.

My answer is this: Too many girls these days are pressured into the role of aspiring doctor or lawyer or Wall Street trader. As a result, the ranks of faerie princesses are declining at an alarming rate.

This is why I'm tickled, well, pink about *Sesame Street*'s newest female Muppet. She's an enthusiastic and unrepentantly feminine little pixie by the name of Abby Cadabby. Abby is a "girly girl" character to contrast the show's rambunctious tomboy Zoe and bilingual guitar-playing Rosita.

Don't get me wrong; I'm a big proponent of gender equality. My parents firmly instilled in me the values of feminism. At the wise age of four, I told the McDonald's cashier that asking if I wanted a "boy toy" or a "girl toy" was sexist.

I then chose the Hot Wheels car.

I think girls should be encouraged to look beyond gender roles but not to automatically shun anything considered "girly." Parents who are overly concerned about their little girls turning into airheaded Barbie wannabes aren't necessarily helping them. What's wrong with a pretty-in-pink girl who dreams of designing sparkly tutus for Chihuahuas...but also might want to be a brain surgeon when she grows up?

Abby, who has just moved to Sesame Street from Fairyland, is enthusiastic without a cheerleader's "rah-rah" or the diva tendencies of a certain tiny Disney faerie. Yet she is decidedly girly, an adjective which cannot be applied to any of the show's other characters. *Sesame Street*, which is going into its 37th season, somehow has no high-profile female lead. Abby Cadabby could change that.

As someone who grew up with *Sesame Street* (and preferred Bert and Ernie to the saccharine Barney), I trust the ever-PC folks over at Sesame Workshop to handle Abby well. They won't let her turn into a walking stereotype. At the same time, I'm glad to see a puppet who clearly embraces her femininity...instead of neutralizing it with gender-ambiguous personality traits.

Maybe the introduction of Abby Cadabby will encourage a few more little (and not-so-little) girls to become aspiring faerie princesses.

WHAT I SEE AND HEAR

A lot has happened in the world since Sasha wrote this as a high school student. Girl power has been reinvented in countless ways, including the explosion of popularity of performers such as Beyoncé and Taylor Swift. Even the iconic Barbie has received a thousand makeovers and starred in a feminist blockbuster of a movie. Nonbinary expressions of gender have become more public, and more accepted.

I notice that the writer begins with an object, a tiara. That is the first clue to help us understand her complex view of the world, but it grows from there. The focus is on a new female Muppet to join the gang on *Sesame Street* (though if I were coaching Sasha, I would politely remind her that a certain diva known as Miss Piggy always had a high profile on *The Muppet Show*). Throughout the essay, Sasha's voice is empowered by word choices that offer the audience things we can see, or at least imagine. My favorite is the idea that there's a girl out there who might design sparkly tutus for Chihuahuas.

This is a great example of that quality in essays that I call spirit. It's as though the writer is answering big questions such as: What do you really care about? What is your passion? When you dream about what you would like to become, what does that look like?

(Sasha Black went on to graduate from the University of California, Berkeley, with a degree in anthropology. Sasha earned a master's degree in education and teaches first grade at a school in Oakland.)

My Church

By Brandon McFarland

(552 words)

I love church. From the screaming organ, to the church mothers in big hats, to the peach and teal polyester choir robes. It's always fun to watch a 250-pound man doing the church rock in one of those.

For me, being at church is like walking into an episode of *Cheers*—you know, everybody knows your name. But for a whole year, I was missing. I got a job that required me to work long hours on weekends. You can't announce that over the pulpit. "Brandon's got a job, y'all, so he's not going to be coming through." So, to my church family, I was there one day, and then, "poof!"

I felt sort of guilty being a no-show. Growing up, I didn't pray regularly throughout the week—I would try to cram it all into Sunday. With my truancy from church, I felt the fear of somehow losing my religion and the guilt of being an inert Christian. So my mom became my church. She told me you can never lose what God has put in you, and as long as I set aside personal time to read the Bible, then I'd be cool—guilt free.

Every time I had read the Bible in the past, I would start yawning and rubbing my eyes. I had never read anything in that good book that held my attention, that I could relate to. But after about four months of my mom being on my back, I finally opened up the book of Proverbs. The first couple of scriptures had me hooked. King Solomon sits a group of young men down and proceeds to basically tell them, "When you see a loose woman, run in the opposite direction!" Word?! It was the first time the Bible had ever made me laugh.

After a while, I started feeling like I was in church when I wasn't...kind of like being in an empty sanctuary all by myself. Reading the words on my own made me relate more to the Bible than staring at some guy break it down. More important, I used to only pray when I was in trouble, like most people do: "God, I need you to pay these bills for me." But I started to pray all week long, whenever I needed to get stuff off my chest.

A year later, I quit the job, and my first reaction was to wake up and go to church. Even though I had reached this new understanding of God, I realized spirituality is only part of what makes church so important. It's also a chance to be with all my blood relatives, and almost 300 others who have known me since I was born and treated me like family ever since. Let me do the math—that means I got like 50 grandmothers, 100 uncles, and countless cousins. And 20 girlfriends. If there were no building, church would be in the park, or in the street—wherever the people are. And the Bible's no substitute for that.

But I actually had to leave church to realize salvation won't come from my parents or extended family. They talk about Jesus and become joyous and loud. I'm not there yet, although I have a praise report — I'm making progress, developing a personal relationship with God.

WHAT I SEE AND HEAR

Although this was written as a radio piece, it would not be hard to translate this into a college essay. Brandon is a young Black man who writes with passion and humor about his life and his culture. I am not suggesting that there is a white or Black or Asian or Hispanic style of writing — or a male or female or nonbinary style of writing. I'm merely suggesting that what readers care about is authenticity, especially when they "hear" it in the voice of the writer.

The Black Church is an important part of American history and culture, and I applaud the way that Brandon filters it through his own family and experience.

There is a tension here, in which his retreat from church is challenged by his mother, whom he wants to please. The writer turns out to be a young man willing to figure things out: his faith, his family, and the importance of his community.

I admire the way he brings us into the church, describing the people and the energy of the ritual. His exploration of the wisdom of Solomon made me laugh, too. The use of quotations brings the prose to life. There is the voice of a real person here in the writing, and a spirit that springs from faith, but goes beyond. This is someone I would want as a member of my student body.

(Brandon McFarland went on to build a career as a sound engineer, composer, and podcaster, currently with Vox Media. It turns out that sound and voice can grow into a vocation.)

Even though the next two essays were not written for radio or audio, they both express that writing quality we are calling voice. We found the first one in an old file without the name of the writer. Even though he is anonymous, there are many things we can learn about his personality, character, interests, quirks, and intelligence. For brevity, we have edited the essay, which we have titled "Doing Your Own Stunts." The original version was exactly 499 words. It began with a complaint that his parents were dragging the writer to a corny Renaissance fair, for which he expresses disdain. Until this:

As I walked into the weapons booth, a large, burly-looking man covered in leather armor and dozens of knives walked up to me. I noted that he looked like the kind of person who could watch *American Gladiators* and wonder why the entire cast was wearing church clothes.

"Twenty percent off on armor, ten percent off on knives. My swords are so sharp, they'll cut an entire wretched dragon in half!" the man yelled about a foot away from my face, followed by some kind of unintelligible ranting about a man named Eddy, who owed him money. The smell of garlic and liquor that had just been blasted into my face seconds before by the surly Renaissance carny nearly overpowered me as I tried to keep my composure.

As I was slowly backing up from the man in the weapons booth, something caught my eye. It was a full-fledged, 42-inch, blood-red katana sword. I had been dreaming about owning a katana for weeks, so seeing it there was love at first sight. I immediately inquired about the sword, to which the man responded by placing it in my hands. "Try it before you buy it. You won't regret it," the man said. I felt like an old-timey ninja back in feudal Japan. I felt the heft of it in my hand, walked to the payment counter, and instantly knew that I was going to buy it.

Things didn't go as planned. No sooner than I had said the words "I'll take it," the blade fell out of the, as it turned out, faulty sheath, and was heading for the ground. That shining piece of steel perfection was suddenly the most important thing in my life, so without thinking, I tried to save the blade from the horrors of the dirt floor by attempting to catch it with my right hand.

A severed nerve, a nicked tendon, and about a minute later, I came to with a towel wrapped around my hand, a half dozen tourists surrounding me with camera phones raised, and a very sweaty carny dragging me through the dirt towards a medical tent while yelling "Move! We got another one!" It was then, in the most ridiculous moment of my life, that, among all of the things going on around me, I somehow remembered that I was wearing my favorite T-shirt. It said, simply, "I do all my own stunts."

WHAT I SEE AND HEAR

I wish I had the writer's name so I could reach out to him and share the joy I experienced from reading this essay again. On the surface, there is not much here that might suggest great academic success in the future. There are no intellectual allusions, no bragging about personal achievements, no professional aspirations. Just a young person who has an accident at a Renaissance fair.

On a second read, however, I notice a writer who is curious and passionate about history, particularly of the Renaissance period, with special knowledge of ancient weaponry and the kind of sword samurai warriors might use.

His essay has a strong narrative line, a memorable setting. As for a writing voice, it's spiced with a bit of snark — the writer looks down on the carny until the carny gets to look down on him! Read this aloud and you can hear the voice of an interesting, somewhat cynical, but self-deprecating writer, someone who has already come to understand the value of a kicker: the word or phrase that lights up the ending of a good story: a T-shirt that reads "I do all my own stunts."

Hold that story in mind as you read the following essay,

which helped get the writer, Holden Strub, into Tulane University. Spoiler alert: He, too, cuts his hand!

The World of the Kitchen

By Holden Strub

(628 words)

There is one place on this planet that I feel utterly content: the small and cramped kitchen in the back of SE Restaurant on the Lower East Side of Manhattan. SE is a restaurant that I worked in during the spring of my junior year in high school. The kitchen is stuffed behind two small metal doors in a windowless stretch behind the dining room, and nothing from the outside permeates those doors. The place is about thirty feet by fifteen feet, but imagine if you put in a dozen full grown adults, thousands of cooking utensils, industrial appliances, and tons of food — the whole place becomes impossibly confining. It can feel almost physically hard to breathe. Yet in this chaos I found profound comfort in the ability to shut my mind off from the rest of the world because God knows I was physically away from it.

When I first walked through those double doors to the kitchen, I was immediately overwhelmed. Bewildered and inexperienced, I was told to peel one hundred potatoes in thirty minutes. I saw it as relatively tedious, but I wanted to impress everyone, so I got to work. Around my thirtieth potato, I started to become distracted as I was entranced by the franticness of this new world around me. I was quickly brought back to the task at hand when a sharp tug informed me I had peeled my finger and not the potato. Soon all those peeled potatoes had a nice speckling of blood. I immediately felt very embarrassed. I was also shocked when the chef told me that in the kitchen "medical aid" is putting tape over any injury and then putting a glove on top of that so as not to spill blood and spoil more food. Then you have to go finish your shift.

My accident showed me how distracting this bubble of pure sensory overload could be. Whether it is the sound of food being chopped or the smell of fresh soup or the sight of bloody red meat or the taste of burning-hot steak or even the feel of ice-cold fish being taken from the cooler, my whole body was absorbed by this tiny backroom world.

My first shift finished with the "family meal," where the cooks made a meal for each other. During the meal I saw I was not alone. Every cook's hands were mostly scar tissue. They wore it proudly, like tattoos. My accident had gained me entry into their ranks—at first, I was the new guy, but now I was one of them.

The next couple months, this place became a haven. I would leave all my worldly troubles on the other side of the small metal doors and devote my time to the kitchen. The cooks helped me hone my culinary skills until I felt I had always been a part of their hardworking family. If I was ever under severe stress from the outside world (like thinking about my future), the cooks would become a motley crew of therapists and help me in whatever odd ways they could. It made me feel welcome, like I was their brother. I was always relaxed and happy there, content even after working ten-hour shifts without sunlight. The world outside the kitchen was irrelevant.

The restaurant changed how I viewed joyfulness. I found that when I was absorbed in something, it was where I found contentment. I had not expected such a reward from cooking, but through the hecticness of the kitchen, I found myself happy. From what I can see now, life (and college) is full of obligations and challenges, but if I can find my two metal doors and work hard, then I can find contentment in whatever I do.

WHAT I SEE AND HEAR

This essay reminds me of an important human and literary truth: Every scar has a story hiding behind it. Think of the lightning bolt scar on Harry Potter's forehead. What is so interesting is the way the word *scar* can work on two different levels. It can be something you can see and perhaps feel with your eyes and hands. You can have a physical scar from, say, an auto accident. But there may also be an emotional scar, a lasting mark on your heart or soul.

I love the way this symbolism appears in two scenes: the

potato peeling scene, and then the dinner where all the cooks prepare a meal for each other.

That gets me to a second important writing strategy: the microcosm, or little world. To get a handle on some big ideas, many writers opt for the strategy of writing about something small. That means that a story about teenage homelessness can be focused on a single automobile where a family is living. Or a story about a life-altering injury might be set in a locker room, or a hospital room, or your backyard. For this writer, the little world is a bustling kitchen in a New York restaurant, full of energy, details that appeal to the senses, and common humanity.

And notice how this writer's voice differs from that of the young man who cut his hand at the fair. The kid who "does his own stunts" prides himself on his cool independence — until he needs the community to rescue him. Holden enters his own world with an open mind, eager to meet and learn from others. This is not to say that Holden's voice is better or more effective. Each young writer, I would argue, discovered the writing voice that helped them narrate the story that only they could tell.

IDENTITY, VOICE, AND RACE

In 2023, the Supreme Court of the United States banned colleges and universities from using race as a determining factor in selecting a student. This was widely considered an end to what was long termed affirmative action. Creating a diverse student body (or workplace) is a noble goal, and many were disappointed when the Court struck down an important tool for getting there.

It turns out there is an alternate path. In large measure, it involves a student's essay. Journalist Jordan Weissmann offers this take in the newsletter *Semaphor*:

> The Supreme Court officially struck down the use of affirmative action in college admissions.... But at the tail end of his decision, Chief Justice John Roberts appeared to leave a path open for schools to continue factoring in race when picking students.
>
> "Nothing in this opinion should be construed as prohibiting universities from considering an applicant's discussion of how race affected his or her life, be it through discrimination, inspiration, or otherwise," Roberts writes.
>
> The caveat is already attracting widespread attention, including from the White House. President Biden seized on Roberts's line in a speech after the decision, urging colleges to adopt a "new standard, where colleges take into account the adversity a student has overcome when selecting between qualified applicants" — including factors like poverty and racial discrimination.

An article in the *New York Times* included interviews with students of color who decided to revise their essays to include more specific information about their race, ethnicity, and heritage. In time, I think we will be able to identify the difference between weaker essays with the intent to announce race from those that tell powerful stories about the experience of race and how the experiences have shaped the writers as students, citizens, and human beings. It's never about just being member of a group; it is about writing the story only you can write about your experience — of discrimination or inspiration — as part of that group.

Many students write about overcoming adversity, and not just on matters of race. That theme is often the focus of writing prompts used in college applications.

As we will see in further examples of student essays, the ability to confront and the effort to overcome obstacles help create a compelling narrative, whether the focus is on race, ethnicity, gender, poverty, disability, or less daunting but still common things that stand in our way.

Throughout the centuries, literature has portrayed the struggle against seemingly impossible odds. Shakespeare can be our guide. Romeo and Juliet hope their love will overcome the hatred of their feuding families. King Lear must face the treachery of two of his three daughters. Rosalind is banished and flees to the Forest of Arden.

While overcoming adversity may be an opportunity to write, it is not a requirement for a personal essay. Remember the young man who finds his identity in the congested kitchen of a New York restaurant. Remember Brandon, who may not be able to attend his church but allows his religious spirit to grow through scripture. And think of my addiction to that arcade game! All of these have some creative tension in them, which can be a liberating substitute for overcoming adversity.

PART VII

Anthology of Student Stories

From this section you can learn:

* How various writers solve the problems presented by a list of prompts
* What diversity looks like within a creative group of young writers
* How to appreciate a good essay
* How to recognize ways a good essay might become better

REFLECTIONS ON STUDENT ESSAYS

In the fall of 2023, I was invited to visit, via Zoom, a class at the University of Texas at Austin, one of the best-regarded public universities in America. It was a class for students interested in public communication. We anticipated that it would attract students already interested in the practical uses of reading and writing. We talked about the writing process, about the difference between reports and stories, and how to make something both clear and interesting. In fact, we covered a number of important subjects that have been described in this book.

At the end of the class, I told them about my work on the personal essay, and invited them to share with me the essays they had written as part of their applications to the University of Texas. Those essays were good enough to help get them accepted, which is all you can ask. With great generosity, several students sent me their essays, along with the hope that reading them might help many future students just like you to get into the school of your choice.

Here they are, followed by my comments. (I have made the occasional small correction in student work, fixing a typo or adding clarifying punctuation. Also, these essays came without titles, so, for fun, I provided them, based on language from the text.)

Color Me Curious

By Abigail Breyfogle

(614 words)

"What is the national dish of Puerto Rico?" "How did oyster crackers get their name?" "What is the difference between white and brown eggs?" Such simple questions fill long car rides with family and restless meals with friends. While this chatter of "whys" and "hows" may seem insignificant, the questions burn in my mind until I find an answer.

This thirst for knowledge seems to be hereditary. While I often scour the web to find solutions, my family finds other ways to satisfy their information cravings. With my father's nightly info dump over his latest podcast listen, or my mother's impeccable assistance during my attempts at *New York Times* crosswords, even questions I didn't know I had are answered. This familial connection extends beyond my immediate family. Some of my brightest memories are of watching *How It's Made* with my grandfather or listening to my grandmother's detailed teachings on alcohol inks, watercolor art, and interior design.

This quest to know more has paid off in unexpected ways. While talking with my mom last spring en route to a UIL competition focused on the Olympics, she mentioned briefly her admiration for an athlete that made history for being the first Olympian gymnast to earn a perfect score. I quickly looked for more information and discovered Romanian gymnast Nadia Comăneci, whose country of origin helped get my team to state.

This year, in my art historical methods class, I have developed my research skills further through the lens of an art historian. When assigned a project where I was able to explore a personal interest, I chose photojournalism, a subject I have felt deeply connected to since joining the yearbook staff. Due to my history of research, I knew which databases to use for reliable sources of famous photographers. I landed upon Dorothea Lange, a figurehead in humanizing the Great Depression through her works such as "Migrant Mother." As I knew my peers had little knowledge of photography, I focused my presentation on a piece that showed obvious photographic composition. It allowed me to share all I learned, and any prior knowledge, to more than just myself.

My ability to analyze sources of information has taken on a greater purpose lately. I can't look at the first search result that auto-populates on Google, or believe every TikTok video that pops up on my "for you" page. I now feel a larger responsibility. The battle of rumor versus fact often hits close to home. When a friend recently told me a story of gang initiation she had heard about from her mother, I looked deeper. Yet I was only met with talk of urban legend. This simple story caused mass panic among my friends, highlighting the potentially destructive power of information. It helped reinforce a valuable lesson. That while information can be beautiful, many dangers can lurk close behind.

While some of my curiosities take less than a few minutes, questions such as "What are the Commonwealth Games?" and "Why is Mahraganat rap illegal?" have led me down rabbit holes of important contemporary events. My quest for knowledge has taken me through twists and turns with interviews and feature stories detailing rock climbing champions, charity organizers, and Texas governor candidate Beto O'Rourke. But it has also made me develop a sense of responsibility. Whether found online, in conversations with family members and friends, or in conducting interviews, information provides me with a deep sense of connection to the world around me. The world is larger than just myself, and with information, I am able to understand the importance of the interconnected web of which I am a piece and the responsibility of sharing these truths with others.

WHAT WORKS

There is a problem that all writers of personal essays face: how to offer a good impression of themselves without bragging too much.

When I read this essay, I thought that this writer strikes exactly the right tone. She doesn't exactly say this: "I am a really curious person who craves information." Yet that might be seen as a theme or focus of the essay. What makes this essay work for me are the numerous and various examples she offers that show us the kind of curious person she is.

She begins in a family setting but quickly moves beyond that to illustrate her range of interests in an academic environment, from a photographer of the Depression to a style of rap music that is banned by the Egyptian government. She caps it off with a brief discussion of the dangers of misinformation. If you check back on all the elements of the essay, they fit together and build to an important conclusion. That effect is what we call coherence.

If I'd had the chance to coach her, we would have taken a look at the length of her paragraphs. Perhaps she might have divided a couple of long ones in half, creating the white space that makes reading a bit easier.

My Curly Monster

By Analise Pickerrell

(572 words)

We all have our monsters. Some are more difficult to get away from than others. But what do you do if your monster is attached to the top of your head? I glared at my reflection, tears streaming down my face, hot iron in one hand, brush in the other, and pure determination in my heart. Mangled and puffy hair extended in every direction except down. But no matter how many times I tempted my curls with the blistering intensity of the heat, they would not be tamed.

The sting of failure spread throughout my whole body. My freshman self felt like the world was crumbling at the foundations. Any hope of hiding the feral lion's mane that was my hair had vanished. And I was absolutely crushed. Devastated at the reality that I was destined to stick out when it seemed as if the only way I could ever be content was to conform. To be like the other high school girls with flawless, pencil-straight locks was equitable to paradise in my mind. But no amount of heat damage stood a chance against the oddness of my biology. My parents could not even reason how their genes had managed to produce me— my thick, blond ringlets in comparison to my mother's dark waves and father's brunette tufts. To say my hair is big would be an understatement, and most do not fail to remind me of this on the daily.

As time went on, it seemed my hair continued to grow exponentially outward. "How is it possible to have this much hair?" "How do you brush it?" "Can I touch it?" These were the questions that plagued my childhood and beyond. In elementary school, rubbing tap water from the school bathroom to conceal my frizz was my go-to technique. Later I evolved to the infamous tight ponytail which I believed limited the volume to some extent. When I finally mastered handling a hot iron, that became my main weapon to conceal my differences.

But no matter how hard I tried to hide my identity this way, my differences always seemed to overpower the efforts I made. It came to a point where the incessant distress exceeded what I could handle. I couldn't restrain something that seemed to have a separate mind of its own. And I finally gave in to the monster.

Letting go of control changed everything. I felt like the chains of insecurity had broken and a weight had been hoisted off of my shoulders. There was nothing holding me back from reaching the potential I had always prevented myself from venturing into. No fear that people would find out what I truly was. And I finally approached the conclusion that the differences that always struck me as a disadvantage and vulnerability, in reality, were my source of strength.

Learning to love what made me uncommon stretched to every area of my life. I finally pursued acting despite the fear that I would be ridiculed for it. I began expressing myself in how I dressed and the interests I invested my time into. I learned to identify with my quirks and eccentric personality. And most importantly, I inspired others to give up control and find the value in their lack of similarity too.

I was never able to get rid of my monster. But I didn't want to. Because it was not a monster anymore — it was my monster.

WHAT WORKS

That first sentence grabbed this book's editor, Talia, by the throat. She was eager to read on to find out more about the monster. On the other hand, the word *monster* threw me off at first. I wondered if it was too strong a word to use for a head of hair you may not like. (This is coming from a bald man, who would cherish any form of hair revival — the bushier, the better.) Then it occurred to me that hair is so much a part of our presence to the world, at times the first thing people notice, that not loving your hair, or being ridiculed for your hair, is an honest problem for many people, with implications related at times to race and ethnicity.

What works well for me is what I will call the circle or ring structure: The end reminds you of the beginning. But along the way a transformation has occurred. She can now claim ownership of her embarrassing feature and embraces it as something distinctive. It's an old story type. Sometimes a blessing (such as winning the lottery) becomes a curse (if it leads to family strife or overspending), but the curse can also become a blessing. Remember that Rudolph's nose gets him treated like an outcast until it becomes the glowing headlight to Santa's sleigh.

What is missing from the essay is the nature of the turning point. When and why did she let go of trying to control what she perceived as a problem? As a coach I would ask her that. Perhaps someone complimented her hair, or perhaps she saw a person with wild hair who acted with a lot of confidence.

My Cross to Bear

By Pili Saravia

(736 words)

I fall asleep every night with my hand clutching my chest, searching for something else to grasp. I used to hold the cross necklace my dad gave me when I was five years old. The necklace has broken multiple times since he gave it to me and despite my best efforts to fix it, it is now beyond repair. The remnants of the necklace sit in my backpack. I miss it and the comfort it brought. Whether my mind was overflowing with euphoria or tortured by memories and fear, I would clutch my necklace each night, knowing I was not alone. The fragments of the gold chain remind me to be present in the moment because nothing lasts forever. I know I have to move on because everything breaks in the end.

One year after my dad gave me the necklace, he died — "in a peaceful way." I can no longer remember if my family members actually told me that, or if I have just turned it into a melody that plays over and over in my brain, trying to convince myself that his last moments with us were pretty. I do remember when my mom told me he wasn't coming back, and how I did not know what that meant until I saw my sister Monica run to hug my mom. I could not understand why that was my last Christmas with him or how our lives would ever continue without him. At six years old there is just so much you do not know; everyone understood that.

Ten years later, my life is completely different. One month after he died, we moved from Mexico to Houston, but no one told me why. I did not know any English, and I cried every day for weeks trying to fit in at school.

The one thing that stayed consistent was our yearly summer trip to our family ranch in Mexico. Like the cross around my neck, a cross stands on the side of the road that leads to our ranch. I have always used that white wooden cross as a checkpoint to know I'm almost home. That cross is anticipation, familiarity, and imagination.

This year, I learned something that changed everything. My mom told my sister and me that my dad was actually taken and held for ransom for a week. My family did everything they were supposed to, and he was finally released. My mom rushed us to my grandma's house with all my aunts and uncles so we could welcome him home from this horrible ordeal. Instead, when he was almost home, they shot him and left him on the side of the road. The spot where he died is where that familiar cross stands.

This year, the cross is danger, lies, and the hole in the bottom of my stomach. We drive past it with guilt for driving down the road he will never be able to take again. Yet, unexpectedly enough, that guilt turned to gratitude. I got out of the car to hug my family, realizing I was surrounded by the people who raised my father. I felt like I was falling into a safety net as I took in the fact that — even through the week of torturous anticipation and the horrible months that followed — everyone in that room lied for ten years just to protect me. Now I understand how strong and incredibly considerate my mom is to have created that temporary world for us. That night, I started a diary which documents only the good parts of everyday life because we are the only ones who can control how our minds think. I realized the importance of holding on to the memories because, again, nothing lasts forever.

Since I started writing this essay a month ago and up until today, I have broken and fixed my cross necklace yet again, not once but twice. I watched as it clung to my body when the shower pressure should have washed it down the drain. I somehow heard it hit the linoleum in the crowded, noisy school hallway. I felt it in my pocket as the only thing that did not get lost when I changed clothes in a mall fitting room. I now know how special it is and that as long as I hold on to it, one way or another, it will hold me in return forever.

WHAT WORKS

Bad things happen to every human being. They may not come as dramatically and destructively as the murder of a parent, but they will come. I am not being cynical when I say that what is bad for the person is sometimes good for the writer. Martin Luther King Jr. wrote his famous letter as a prisoner from the Birmingham jail. One morning in 2015, my wife received two phone calls at the same time, one on her cell, the other on her landline. One informed her that she had been diagnosed with breast cancer, the other that her mother had just died. I have written the story of her nine years of cancer treatment on the pages of my local newspaper several times, receiving thanks from other cancer patients and survivors. Writing about it helps me, and readers tell me it helps them.

Stories of suffering and deaths of family members can be difficult to read. This writer strikes exactly the right tone. The story of the murder of her father comes as a surprise, not just for her, but for her readers. She finds a strong way to symbolize her loss and continuing vulnerability. She begins by presenting us an object with a story hiding inside it, one of my favorite writing devices. The cross—a symbol that is both religious and personal—is broken, seemingly beyond repair. She faces a bigger cross in Mexico, marking the place where her father was shot down. Now knowing the truth, she is inspired to repair the jewelry cross and to own it anew, as a talisman for the enduring love of her family.

If I were coaching the writer, I would encourage another draft, devoted to a single purpose, cutting needless words from sentences, so the hardworking words stand out.

For example, the sentence "I felt like I was falling into a safety net as I took in the fact that — even through the week of torturous anticipation and the horrible months that followed — everyone in that room lied for ten years just to protect me" might become "I fell into this safety net, realizing, even after months of tortured anticipation, that they had all lied for ten years just to protect me." A forty-two-word sentence tightens to twenty-five words, with the best words now more visible to the reader.

Eight Minutes in El Paso

By Claire Schulter

(648 words)

Journalism is dying. Becoming obsolete in a world where the image of a newspaper being thrown over a picket fence seems archaic. This is the response I get from friends, family, and actual strangers when I tell them I plan to pursue journalism. The word "outdated" is the kiss of death in a society wholeheartedly focused on whatever is the best, the shiniest, but most importantly, the newest.

Growing up, I had an affinity for vinyl records,

starting with an old copy of *Rumours* by Fleetwood Mac. Affinity quickly became obsession, with shelves overflowing with records, ranging anywhere from ABBA to Harry Styles. A question often arises about my love for vinyl records: you have a Spotify account, what is the point of having records?

There is a reason that vinyl records are having a renaissance, from a logical standpoint the grooves on records allow for a richer and higher-quality sound, but from a more emotional standpoint, the music just feels different. There is a warmth and a connection that only comes from dropping a needle onto a record, this feeling is unable to be replicated with digital music platforms.

Writing is unique. Writing is one of the only things that is unable to be outsourced. No computer program, no line of code will ever be able to convey a narrative that drips with emotion and humanity in the same way that no Spotify playlist will ever be able to match the sweetness of an album on a record player.

In an age of widespread polarization, I continuously hear that our society is losing the ability to debate, that it too is becoming obsolete. I will not say that this notion is ridiculous, I hold strong convictions, and seeing alternative perspectives proved difficult for me. Finding a middle ground was called outdated, traded in for unmovable pillars in schools of thought.

My freshman year I joined my school's debate team,

I delved into international issues, geopolitics, and policy issues and with that truly began to inform myself about the world around me. I could see my perspectives changing, my worldviews radically shifting.

During my sophomore year, I was chosen to debate on the United States Development Team, where 15 underclassmen are chosen to represent the US from applicants across the country. I spent what felt like endless hours training, writing, and speaking. Hundreds of speeches later, I could feel my worldview changing again.

El Paso, Texas. Such an odd place to have a revelation. Standing in a high school classroom I began my state finals speech. Knowing for the next eight minutes my words mattered more than they ever had before. I needed to speak precisely, my words needed to cut through the room and resonate with the panel of seven judges I had sitting before me. Seven people who had lived completely different lives than me, I needed to reconcile the differences and make them care about the things I had to say if only for eight minutes.

Standing on an auditorium stage, I was handed a state championship trophy, an accumulation of so much training and so many sleepless nights and all I could think about was that connection. My words had connected to these strangers and pulled at something inside of them. I believe that words have unparalleled power, and have the power to connect anyone to each other. Even as divided as people can be, debate will never become impossible as long as we use language to connect to each other.

Journalism, debate, and even something as silly as records have all been called obsolete. I don't think I believe in obsolete. It is all about connection. Vinyl connects me to music, my words connect me to the world. Even though the art of debate is changing, even though journalism is changing, there is no such thing as "obsolete" when there is a connection.

WHAT WORKS

While reading this essay for the first time, I began to worry. It felt like three essays. One about the writer's desire to pursue journalism. Another about a whimsical attachment to vinyl records. And yet another about a wonderful achievement in a state debate competition. How will the writer connect these, or will she? It was a similar feeling I have when I watch the final episode of a long dramatic streaming series on Netflix, and I notice there is only a half-hour left. I worry about whether they will weave the threads together for a successful conclusion.

What I needed from the writer were better transitions between the three key elements of obsolescence. Without them, the reader may feel that something crucial to understanding is missing. In the end, our writer knew what she needed to do. In a nifty final paragraph, she ties all three elements together: journalism, debate, and vinyl recordings. All three work together to create a crucial theme, that what some folks call obsolete may have enduring meaning for individuals and society.

And I smiled with appreciation of her use of detail, naming three bands/performers from her record collection. Perhaps she might have described just one classic album cover to appeal to our visual appetite. One more thing: the essay needs just a bit of proofreading. She makes her meaning clear, but she sometimes squeezes two sentences into one without the best punctuation, as in "There is a reason that vinyl records are having a renaissance, from a logical standpoint the grooves on records allow for a richer and higher-quality sound, but from a more emotional standpoint, the music just feels different." A colon, semicolon, or, my preference, a period after *renaissance* would help lock the box.

A Good Egg

By Eva Yakubov

(643 words)

An old, frail Moldovan woman stood with an egg in one hand, determined, advising me to sit down in front of her. My mother and grandmother act as observers, standing on the other side of the dimmed room. How are a woman and an egg supposed to heal years' worth of rock and decay buried deep in my throat? The woman places the warm egg on my forehead and spins it subtly as she asserts for me to stay quiet.

For this decay to diminish, a hard-boiled egg and a woman who specializes in home remedies didn't seem like a probable solution for a 13-year-old girl. Perhaps this was probable for the swarms of Eurasian women who believed a warm egg could capture the essence of fear, or this stutter. But to me, this moment felt like a capital X on all hope of getting across a word starting with any of the 21 consonants.

Ever since my family and I immigrated from Israel to America, for most of my childhood as I learned English, words always felt restrained. Buried at the tip of my tongue, a shadow would lie, surfacing out when attempting to communicate. My mind was creating a false illusion toward every set of eyes that looked my way. Before I could tell it to stop, it had penetrated the linings of my lips to form the product of a slow mutter. The idea of control seemed improbable, as did the remedies that the Moldovan woman proposed or the tactics of my elementary school speech pathologists. Despite this, I had the desire to be heard and to freely share my perspective on the world.

I realized there were various ways I could openly express myself without feeling trapped when a certain phrase wouldn't come out as intended. I noticed that the fear linked to my hindrance of speech decreased with the time and thought I put into creative expression, specifically, through personal projects.

I sought out interests such as poetry. Something that had previously brought me little interest, was now a new sense of comfort I never knew I needed. When spoken words wouldn't transpire, I could fall back to writing as a prospect. I never viewed poetry as an art form that required a level of proficiency which, to me, made it one of the greatest things. This proved that I didn't need great oral proficiency because I had the power of even greater communication through the simplicity of a couplet.

With each free verse I write, my world begins to unravel just the way that I imagine it in my head. By fueling my passion, I was again able to understand myself. Communication was less limited when I could fill the space in my mind, rather than feed into the borders, inclined on lined paper. After becoming more comfortable in my presence, I looked for ways to stretch beyond my personal space.

My freshman year, I was invited to stand in front of a crowd of over 200 people to give a reading at Rice University. One year prior, there was no way I would have agreed to the offer. However, I found myself feeling at ease with the idea. At that moment, I was able to share a poem that encompassed my culture, something I was previously hiding. The reading showed me that I was capable of expression for much longer than I was allowing myself. My thoughts drew me back to the Moldovan woman's purpose. I doubted the egg just like my own voice, but over time, the egg evolved into a symbol of confidence, stripping away the fear that once took hold of me. From then on, I wouldn't allow myself to be held back by the disposition of my physical surroundings because although they were once my dictator, I was now theirs.

WHAT WORKS

If you want to tell a story, even a short one, you need to create a scene. All the movies you watched, all those sitcoms and rom-coms, your favorite novels of all time — they all are built upon a sequence of scenes. At its smallest, a tiny scene is called an anecdote, a mini-narrative used to exemplify an idea or an emotion.

A type of scene that works in many stories is a ceremony. The novel *The Godfather* begins with a wedding and ends with a baptism; the in-between is punctuated by a sequence of mob murders. All of our lives are marked by ceremonies: birthday parties, proms, first communions and bar mitzvahs, graduation ceremonies, weddings, funerals.

In this essay, our writer begins with a wonderful whimsical unexpected ceremony in which an old woman performs a home remedy, with that great egg, to relieve a young girl of her stutter. It reveals a lot about the writer's problem, but also her spirit and ethnicity. And, of course, it is a kind of ceremony, not quite spiritual, but almost.

There is a ceremony, of sorts, at the end of the essay, a public reading at a university. Speaking in public turns out to be one of the most common human phobias, multiplied many times for a person with a speech disorder.

If I had a chance to work with Eva, I would use the formula I use with every writer — including myself. I begin with "what works" so we can build on that. For example, I liked the fact that the writer brings back the Moldovan woman with the magic egg at the end. On the other side — what needs work — I would ask the writer to consider quoting a line or two from the poem she read, especially if it is relevant to her struggle.

There are other things to attend to: some imprecise language, a couple of puzzling metaphors, and sentences that could be tightened for language and emphasis. That said, it helps to remember that a college essay doesn't need to be perfect: It just needs to get you where you want to go.

This one helped get Eva into the university of her choice.

Editing My Life

By Sofia Alvarado

(707 words)

Ping! I hear the message float on my screen as I've just exiled my phone toward the corner of my bed to at last focus on studying. I already know who sent the message; it's right on time with our routine: 11:30 pm equals a text from my father about his school work. I don't have to check to know it says, "Hija, bajas y mi lees esto rapidito? (Will you come downstairs and edit this for me?)." I throw my equations off my lap and hurry downstairs as I give myself a wake-up pep talk. I meet my dad in our home office as we settle into our natural back and forth.

"I just needed some quick help with this group discussion I need to turn in," he says. I look at his computer and scroll down; it's three pages long. I sigh and grab our spare chair; it's going to be a long one tonight.

I've been editing and proofreading everything my parents have written for as long as I can remember speaking English. Coming from Venezuela with little to no understanding of English, I was proud of the effort they were making now to get MBAs. I was also well aware of how much more work my clients (my parents) would need from me (their freelance copy editor).

A once bi-weekly occurrence became daily. My usual 11:20 bedtime extended into 1:00 am. The abnormally bright light in our home office dried out the contacts in my eyes as I triple-checked the edits I had made. I repeatedly asked my dad to say his ideas out loud in Spanish so I could translate his work, hoping to portray his underestimated intelligence in a language I was far from an expert in myself. My vocabulary expanded as I attempted to decipher and reproduce the minutiae of his word choice from Spanish to English.

My parents finished their degrees in two years, and while the late nights were not missed, that feeling of snapping into that perfect word I needed to shave down a sentence was. My desire to dig through the tangled roots of a paragraph and work with someone to grow their idea into a garden of words persisted. Of course, there was the occasional email. Still, I missed our routine.

Then I found what I was missing. An offhand comment about our school's copy-editing team by a friend spurred me into action. I was instantly intrigued and, minutes later, sought out the sponsor for the team, begging for more information. He enlightened me on the competitions I could enter, and the last one was coming up soon, allowing me to enter at the last minute. So, *AP Style Book* in hand, I started studying. I was excited at the prospect of turning a skill I had unintentionally practiced so much and grown to enjoy into a competitive edge. The competition was only a couple of days away, though, and I was reminded of my experiences dealing with my parents' more complex assignments.

The essays my parents had to write required a much more high-brow understanding of subjects I had a rudimentary knowledge of. However, by stripping ideas into basic building blocks I could sort through, I could quickly learn what was needed, take a minute to apply a more complex understanding, and then assist my parents. This skill began to impact how I approached new concepts, whether in school or watching the news. Through the stressful nights of poring over work I felt ill-equipped to handle, I learned how to deliver a quick turnaround with the information I had mastered mere minutes before. I followed this approach with my competition, reviewing the basics of grammar I felt confident in and then adding on the specificities.

Three days later, I was anxiously pacing a hallway in Klein High School, awaiting the results of my first UIL competition. Ping! A message on my phone. But not a favor; this time, it was recognition for my work, my results from the competition. "You placed 5th out of 18, congrats!" read my sponsor's text. As I read, a shy smile spread across my face as I buzzed with excitement of the opportunities to come.

WHAT WORKS

I love this essay for many reasons. There is an old journalism saying that goes like this: If a dog bites a man, that is not news. But if a man bites a dog, that is news. A parent helping a child with homework is not news. A child helping her parents — that is news.

The writer offers us some dialogue, one of the most

interesting story elements. To reveal her family's cultural heritage and facet of her identity, she includes a bit of Spanish. Such dialogue turns words into action, giving the writer a distinctive voice, with her charming parents acting as backup singers.

But there's much more going on in this essay, another example of the "curse" becoming a blessing. Copyediting her parents was perceived as a chore until she realized that it was a kind of boot camp, an experience that revealed that she was good at an important craft. Part II of the essay shows her taking advantage of her knowledge and succeeding at a craft that is likely to become a career. This journey of self-understanding serves as a great story arc. Though her writing includes some minor errors, she has mastered the semicolon, an underappreciated mark of punctuation.

How About a Fist Bump Instead?

By Maia B. Thomas

(646 words)

Every time someone reaches out their right palm to me with a beaming face expecting to get a friendly handshake, I instantly freeze. They'll think I'm rude or boring if I tell them I don't want to. If I tell them I am unable to, they'll ask why. Would they believe me if I told them I have a disability?

I've always been able to manage life without every stranger giving me a pitying, invasive stare as they walk past me (as many people do to someone who doesn't operate the same way as them). While I'm extremely grateful for this privilege, I am still different. Growing up, I was never fazed by my situation. I didn't even know what I had until I was in seventh grade. No one noticed what set me apart; all I cared about was telling people I was left-handed as an ice-breaker every new school year. But when peers began to notice how weirdly I typed on the computers and that I couldn't do simple choreography for choir shows, it was as if my world was closing in on me.

"But you don't look crippled," one of my classmates remarked when I tried to explain the abnormal curvature of my hand on the keyboard. Comments like this led to an extreme state of confusion and embarrassment about my self-image. I became uncomfortable identifying as disabled because it always felt like a lie. My case was not nearly as severe as others, so why should I consider myself affected at all? In turn, my desire for independence led to an inability to admit that some aspects of life would be more challenging for me.

It wasn't until my junior year of high school that my perspective changed. I began to embrace the idiosyncrasies of my body through playful jokes with close friends who refreshingly treated me like a normal person. Because of this approach, I eventually discovered the bright side of what I used to consider something that should be locked away. In the journey towards being fully comfortable in my own skin, I realized that being open about who I was would be much more effective than trying to imitate those around me. Hiding would only cut me off from the opportunity to experience life in the most vivid sense. I didn't function the same way, and finally, I began to see the beauty in that uniqueness.

This allowed me to further connect with others who felt similar to me and helped me advocate for myself appropriately. No, I can't give a proper handshake or cut a steak at a fancy restaurant, but undoubtedly experiences like these have allowed me to appreciate the clarity with which I see the world.

Looking back on my life, I have always been extremely outspoken about the issues I care about, even when I wasn't confident in my identity. I lost friendships, faced death threats, and was laughed at by the people I was closest to for calling out the terrible treatment of an autistic kid or the harmful speech towards the LGBTQ+ students at my conservative school. Now, some of those same people that I once called out have a changed perspective and I am proud of how my words influenced positive change.

I truly believe that having the unique position of living in and viewing society differently gave me the guts to speak up and is a monumental part of my compassion, empathy, and a clear sense of morality. This strong skill set will seamlessly flow into my contribution to a better community as I continue to grow and learn. Today, I can proudly say that my outspokenness and appreciation for my disability translate into a fierce confidence in who I am and a clear yet gentle sense of the environment around me. I have spastic hemiplegia, can we fist bump instead?

WHAT WORKS

As soon as I finished reading this essay, I searched online for "spastic hemiplegia." I found this quick definition: "a type of cerebral palsy that occurs when the condition of muscle stiffness impacts one full side of the body." If I had been coaching this writer, we might have had a conversation about whether to include a definition such as that. That said, there is a real power in introducing that technical phrase at the very end, in a final short sentence. All of the earlier descriptions, in which the effects of the disability are described, lead up to that final sentence, which could have been even more powerful if split into two sentences: "I have spastic hemiplegia. Can we fist bump instead?" Authors like to save their best thoughts for their shortest sentences, and "can we fist bump instead?" works particularly well as a creative echo of the first sentence about not wanting to shake hands.

For many reasons in life, people come to see themselves as victims. There is a healing process that can follow, when that person sees themselves first as a survivor, and then as an advocate, exactly the journey this writer has taken.

Power of the Image

By Grace R. Gates

(651 words)

I was sitting in the worst possible position for a photographer to be in during a baseball game: the first baseline. Luckily, there would be no 90 mile-per-hour line drives flying in my direction, just a ball slowly rolling by as a 4-year-old ran her hardest to the bag behind me. I decided to spend my Saturday evening photographing this tee-ball game so I would have pictures to submit with my article about youth sports for a local magazine.

Even though the article was about kids, I was much more focused on the job at hand rather than interacting with them. There was one girl in particular, though, that stood out to me. Her blue eyes peeked through dark hair covering her face. She seemed smaller than the rest of the team, partly because she stood three inches shorter than every other girl, and mostly because her confidence level was astonishingly low. When she came up to bat, I felt my excitement grow. I captured every last swing until she finally hit the ball and ran off to first base.

I did this for every other player, of course; though for this one, I turned my camera vertically. This could be my cover shot. On May 3rd, 2022, every grocery store within a 40-mile radius held a copy of the Picayune magazine with "Youth Sports a Home Run" across the front. Below the text, a girl stood mid-swing: a piercing blue gaze on the softball.

I felt nothing but pride as I flipped between the pages, reading my very own article, seeing my very own name beneath the words. After this kickstart to my career, I actually believed that I could do anything. I received congratulations from my friends and family throughout the day, and even the local radio station mentioned my accomplishment.

Late in the evening, though, my phone buzzed with a message that stood out from the rest. The number wasn't saved in my phone, but I knew it came from the parent of the blue-eyed girl on the front cover. I had previously asked permission to use her picture. Three weeks after that exchange, her dad let me know he found a copy of the magazine. It took an additional text to tell me he had also found an incredible amount of encouragement.

The girl on the front cover was adopted by her grandparents after her mom fell into addiction. Her new dad explained that the family was happy, she was safe, but they were having trouble adapting to taking care of a daughter again.

"When she gets bigger and understands what all has transpired, this could really give her encouragement that she can do anything!" he said. "Plus it made me proud! We have really struggled being parents again! God bless you."

In shock, I let him know he was doing a great job, and I was beyond grateful for his vulnerability. When I walked onto that baseball field, my intentions were selfish; I was writing an article to improve my resume, not just inspire kids to play sports. One text message changed my entire perspective. All of the decisions — choosing a game, turning my camera, the editors picking the photo — created an opportunity for me to impact others.

I've always wanted to study journalism: after this experience, I now understood why. Everyone has their own hill to climb, and sharing someone's story can provide enough encouragement to change a life. This opportunity taught me that I can do anything, but it also opened my eyes to the fact that my purpose is bigger than myself. I pray that one day that little girl realizes she too can do whatever she puts her mind to, and understands that nothing goes without purpose. Above all else, the cover featuring that little girl proved to me that every story is invaluable: not just the ones I get to write.

WHAT WORKS

It is easy to see why the writer of this essay got herself accepted into an important collegiate journalism program. She is a talented photographer, and she can write clearly and tell a good story. She is ambitious and wants to succeed. And her essay also reveals something more important: how she has come to understand that a craft — such as writing or photography — is most important when it attaches itself to a noble cause.

I love the genuine humility of the writer describing her more selfish motives for adding to her portfolio and résumé. But then the testimony from the girl's family teaches her the power of her craft, showing her that the good that you do can often surprise you by rising above your intentions.

PART VIII

100 Writing Tools

From this section you can learn:

* Tips and tricks the best writers use to do their best work
* How to use these writing strategies more purposefully
* How to build a workbench to store all your tools, now and into the future

100 WRITING TIPS FOR YOUR
PERSONAL ESSAY

If you have read this far, you know that this book contains many different examples of essays written mostly by high school students applying to college. We are grateful to all the writers, in all their variety, for sharing their work. We all benefit from the values and the tools that they brought to the task, whether or not they got into the school of their choice. As they say in Harry Potter's world, it is more often the case that the wand chooses the wizard, rather than the wizard choosing the wand. I did not get into Princeton, but it turned out that Providence College was the place I needed to be. My school chose me.

What follows is a list of one hundred good writing strategies and habits, many of which I've already touched on, with a few new tricks added for fun.

SETTING THE SCENE

1. Choose a small world after all. Many writers handle big themes by writing about a small place or space where characters interact. The fancy word for this is *microcosm*. *Micro* means "small," as in *microscope*. *Cosm* means "big world," as in *cosmic*. A group of people stranded on an island. A ship at sea. An emergency room. A classroom. A locker room. Remember when our writer described what he learned in that tiny kitchen of a New York restaurant? That is a small world.

2. Start with an inciting incident. Lots of TV cop shows begin with someone discovering a dead body. That launches the action. Hopefully your essay will not start with a corpse, but it can start with a moment of high drama, like the day you discovered you were adopted. Or it can start with a minor event, like that time you walked down the school corridor with a strip of toilet paper stuck to the bottom of your shoe.

USING DETAIL

3. The bigger, the smaller. Your essay will not be ten thousand words, or even one thousand words. Think of that as an advantage. If you want to demonstrate some quality of yours — empathy, courage, curiosity — pick something small that shows your stuff: a photograph, an heirloom, a trophy, an old T-shirt you wear all the time. To prove that my wife loves Christmas, I could list for you the number of holiday decorations she keeps up all year round, or the number of Christmas sweaters she has hanging in the closet, or the piggy bank she devotes exclusively to saving for family members' presents. The point is, it's often the smallest details that have the biggest impact on a reader.

4. Pick an object with a story hiding inside it. Look through the drawers or boxes where you keep your prized possessions or mementos. What is the most "valuable" thing you own? I once wrote an eleven-part newspaper series titled "Sadie's Ring," inspired by a wedding ring given to me by my grandmother. It told the story of how much that ring meant to me, a story about family, love, and heritage.

5. Plant gold coins in your essay. A gold coin is something special: a detail, a quote, a tiny story, a play on words, something that stands out, like when a high school writer compares his skinny legs growing up to those of a daddy longlegs. You almost always need a gold coin at the beginning, and one for the road at the end. Even better if another one is shining in the middle. Imagine you are walking down a forest path at dusk and you look down and see a gold coin and pick it up. In a while you see another. You pick it up, of course. What would you do next? Keep walking until you are sure the coins have run out. Your readers will keep reading, as long as you continue to reward them.

6. Show and tell. It is OK to tell your readers that you are intellectually curious, that you are the most literate person in your extended family (except for your mom), or that you are obsessed with numbers. Please tell us, but also show us. Like in kindergarten: show and tell, or tell and show. If you tell an anecdote about you and a classmate having a long debate about the nature of the number zero, you are showing, not just telling, that math is your academic passion.

USING LANGUAGE

7. Rely on magic numbers. Writers use different numbers of examples for different purposes. If you want a superfocus, use a single example: Beyoncé. If you want a reader to compare and contrast, use two examples: Beyoncé and Taylor Swift. If you want to show the reader that they have all they need to know at the moment, use three examples: Beyoncé, Taylor Swift, and Billie Eilish. One, two, or three, each powerful number sends a secret message to readers.

8. Use a mix of short and long sentences. Long sentences work best when you are taking the reader on a little journey, showing them that your favorite library shelf has a hundred books on it, in historical order, starting with Homer's *Iliad* and ending with Dr. Seuss's *Horton Hears a Who!* The short sentence delivers a sharp truth: You like to read.

9. Take good words or phrases out of hiding. If you have a great detail, a funny bit, important language, you may want to move it from the middle of a sentence or paragraph to the end. I might write, "The Queen is dead, my lord." Shakespeare wrote it better: "The Queen, my lord, is dead," ending with a shock. The thing that makes you laugh in a joke, yes, comes at the end.

10. Pay attention to paragraphs. Even if your essay is only three hundred words, don't deliver it in one long paragraph. One paragraph makes your essay look gray and tedious, hard on the eyes. If you write five hundred words, using two or three paragraphs makes sense: beginning, middle, end. After each paragraph comes white space, making your essay easier to read.

ELEMENTS OF STORY

11. Tell a story. A good essay tells a story, so it needs some of these elements:

- A main character
- Something that happens, set in scenes

- A setting: a time and place where the action occurs
- Dialogue: at least two people speaking aloud
- Chronology: the order in which things happen
- Motivation: why someone chooses to do something
- Resolution: an ending in which something is resolved

Let's break those out in the next examples.

12. Develop your characters. The main character will often be you, since the story is about you. But many of the stories in this book include supporting characters other than the writer. All characters need characteristics, details that separate one person from others.

13. Create scenes. Some scenes, like the time your sailboat sank and you almost drowned, can take up most of an essay. But there can be mini-scenes as well, like that time I lost my wallet and spent an hour in my closet, searching through every pants pocket to find it. During the course of any day, you probably witness lots of little scenes. These can become anecdotes. Watch your favorite sitcom or rom-com. One scene after another.

14. Choose a vivid setting. Think of all the settings you have visited in these model essays: a dusty road to a Mexican ranch, a room where a young woman holds up a trophy, a snorkel shop in Ecuador, a Little League field, a Renaissance fair, the small kitchen in a New York restaurant. Sometimes the setting can be described in just a few words: a city park known for its palm trees, pelicans, and pickleball courts.

15. Let someone else speak. Most stories would be pretty boring if no characters spoke. There are at least two ways to bring more voices into your story, in addition to your own. The first is by quoting someone you use as a source in your story. For example, you might quote the neighbor who comments, "We could not believe that the blizzard buried your father's Mustang convertible." The other way is through dialogue that is part of the story. "Oh, my goodness. Look over there. The storm made Dad's car disappear!" The reader sees a quote, but overhears people speaking to each other.

16. Create closure. The end of your essay can echo your beginning. This happens in movies, novels, and musical compositions. Think of it as a kind of circle structure, sometimes called a "ring." Maybe you describe yourself making a Spam sandwich on pumpernickel in the first paragraph, when you look out the window and see something astonishing. Bringing the reader back to that sandwich — or that window — at the end creates a nice feeling of closure.

17. Plant a clue at the beginning. Water it in the middle. Harvest it at the end. I learned this from reading *The Great Gatsby* about a dozen times. Fitzgerald introduces the symbol of a green dock light in the first chapter and gives it full meaning in the last chapter. But he mentions it in another scene, right in the middle of the book, so you won't forget that light. Even if your essay is only 750 words, there may be a spot in the middle where you can link beginning and end.

WRITING A GOOD LEAD

18. Grab the reader early. You don't have to shock the reader at the beginning: "I'm writing this with tears in my eyes because a tornado destroyed my house yesterday!" But remember your audience, a group of dedicated but busy readers. You should lead with something important or interesting that draws in the reader right away.

19. Start with an anecdote that sparks curiosity to learn more. "It wasn't much of a storm, so why was it raining *inside* my house?"

20. Point to your focus. The lead should reflect the focus of the story—the main thing you want to say—but it does not have to contain all the key elements. Think of your lead, to paraphrase author John McPhee, as a flashlight that points into a dark room. It will encourage the reader to look more deeply into the essay.

YOUR PROCESS

21. Embrace your role as a writer. If you are reading this book, if you are in the process of writing your college essay, you have earned the right to think of yourself as a writer. It's an honor to call yourself a reader and a writer. If you embrace that identity, instead of fearing or dreading it, you will get through this important task and also build a foundation of authorship you can use for the rest of your life.

22. Don't box yourself in early. You've probably heard the advice not to limit yourself to applying only to that one school that you have always dreamed about attending. Apply there. Shoot high. But also look at safe schools where you are more likely to get accepted. In that same spirit of openness, keep an open mind about the topic of your essay. Consider all the options before you focus on one or two.

23. Lower your standards — at the beginning. This advice I learned from poet William Stafford. No essay I have ever written was great, or even good, right from the beginning. Expecting to get it right on the first try only leads to stress and writer's block. Relax, if you can, early in the process. Get your hands moving. Get your thoughts on paper. When you get to a second and a third version, you will raise your standards, almost without trying.

24. Try writing multiple leads. This advice comes from writing coach Donald Murray. Rather than labor over one opening, he encourages writing several — five, six, seven — before choosing the best one. This is not as hard as it might seem. Let's go back and remember Charley Daly's essay (page 26). Given her content, she had lots of choices: "I was born on Valentine's Day with eleven toes." Or "I have something in common with Ernest Hemingway's cat: We were both born with an extra toe." "When I told a friend I was polydactyl — born with an extra toe — they thought I said I was a pterodactyl, a flying dinosaur." Now she has choices, and once she knows what story she wants to tell, she can make a decision based on what is most important or most interesting.

25. Free write. If you get stuck, here's my advice: Just pick a prompt. Any prompt. Maybe the first one. Then sit at the computer and start typing — say for thirty minutes without stopping. At that half-hour mark, get up and take a break and grab a snack. Now go back to your text, read it, maybe print it out. Circle the one or two best things that you like. Maybe put it aside, sit down, and write again. You may find that in that single hour you have launched a successful essay.

26. Don't procrastinate, rehearse. In every writing class I teach, I see some students scribbling away, and others staring into space. Eventually I discovered that the ones who are not on task may not be procrastinating; they may be "rehearsing." They are thinking about what they want to write. If you have ever asked someone for a job or a raise, if you have ever asked someone out on a date or to the prom, you already know how to rehearse. You don't just blurt your proposal, you imagine it, dream about it, chat about it with someone you trust. Now you have the best excuse for anyone who accuses you of procrastinating: "Excuse me. I'll have you know that, with the help of Dr. Clark, I am not slacking off. I am rehearsing."

PICKING YOUR PROMPT

27. Study lots of prompts. Most of the prompts that come from colleges and admissions services are good ones, tested over a long period of time. If you are offered more than one prompt, take a little time and think of what you might write in response to each of them. As you survey them, you are likely to discover that one of them stands out. It may immediately generate a story idea. Or it may point you into a number of useful directions. You don't have to go through them alone. Enlist friends, family, or teachers to help you brainstorm some potential ideas.

28. Use the prompt as an open door, not a narrow window. Many students will write an essay that checks off all the boxes suggested by the prompt. Describe an obstacle (check). Something that happened in school (check). How you overcame it (check). What you learned from it (check). How you think this will help you in college (check). While there is nothing wrong with this approach, it will put you in a pile with more than half of those who are applying. Your readers will recognize the bland pattern and hope for something more interesting from the next writer. Instead, put that checklist aside, and scribble a story that illustrates the focus of the prompt.

29. Don't just make a statement. Tell a story. A statement sounds like this: "I have always wanted to attend the Rhode Island School of Design." A story sounds like this: "When I was a kid, security chased me from the RISD campus for drawing images in colored chalk on the sides of buildings. My favorite was a punk version of Tinker Bell."

30. Remember that a prompt is just a topic. It's your job to turn it into a story. As you read prompts, it will help for you to find one that not only lets you write a good essay, but also one that helps you write to the assigned length: 300, 500, 750 words or more. Don't try to impress the readers by handing in an epic. Longer does not mean better or more meaningful.

31. Look for a topic that will reveal your knowledge. In his essay, Sam French showed readers his interest in theater and popular culture. Emme Slaughter referred to her science idol, Madame Curie. Charley Daly expressed her affinity with Hemingway's six-toed cats. If you have a desire to study a particular academic discipline and you can tell a story that reveals your early interest, by all means do so.

32. Look for a topic that reveals your character — the virtuous parts. My mother used to say "If it's true, son, it is not bragging." If you won that championship, or that trophy, or that recognition, or the key to your city because of your charitable work, you want the admissions committee to know about it. Look for opportunities to mention achievements. It must be said that most of us don't like a braggart, but in a story where you show your virtues, rather than tell them, your achievements will seem more natural and to the point.

33. Show some spirit. The essays I most admire are the ones with a characteristic I call spirit. It's a vague term, like saying that a performer has the "It Factor" or "rizz" (slang for charisma). Let me try to break it down: An essay has spirit if after you read it you want to know more, if you want to meet the writer, if you want to pass along the story to someone else. Bland writing, even if it is accurate, lacks spirit. Spirit is a wonderful word, derived from the Latin *spiritus*, meaning "breath." An essay that breathes feels human, full of life.

RESEARCH AND REPORT

34. Report on your memories. You can think of your essay as a mini-memoir or as a chapter of the mega-memoir you'll be writing fifty years from now. Let's imagine that you want to write an essay about the day that you learned to read. Take a notebook or a yellow pad and just make a list of your memories — where you were, what you were reading, who else was there, how you were feeling. As you make your list, you will see that one memory leads to another. At this point, you don't have to concern yourself about the accuracy of your memory. That can come later as you refresh the memory.

35. Explore old photos, documents, and other key artifacts. The poet T. S. Eliot wrote that he was always looking for the object that represented the idea or emotion he was trying to express. One of the best sources for a good story or essay is an old photo. That image may spark memories you can add to your list. Even better, the photo contains evidence, and specific details. What your haircut looked like, what was hanging on your bedroom wall, how proud you looked in your Wonder Woman jammies. I have been able to write countless essays based upon documents I have saved or discovered. For my generation, this meant yearbooks, autograph books, baby books, medical records, handwritten love letters, newspaper clippings. Paper, paper, paper. In the digital age, these may be text messages, Instagram posts, or your Google Photos archive, but you can still look for things that help tell the story of your young life.

36. Check online resources. The internet offers search resources that my generation could never have imagined. Let's say, for example, that you wanted to write something about your first days in high school. For me, that would have meant September of 1962. A quick search on my phone tells me that in that very same month, JFK promised that Americans would put a man on the moon before the end of this decade (which we did, in 1969). We carry encyclopedias in our pockets; use them.

37. Initiate conversations. One of the best things about writing personal essays is that you can get great material from people who know and care about you, such as parents and grandparents, siblings, coaches, teachers, neighbors. If you tell them you are writing about the only day you remember seeing snow in Florida, you will be surprised at how eager they are to share their memories. Pull out a little notebook, and you have the makings of a fruitful interview.

38. Interview people in the know. You may want to do more formal interviews with experts on the topic you are writing about. In this collection, there are stories about speech disorders, religious traditions, cuisine, sports, gender, race, the natural world, and many other subjects. If I am writing a story about brown pelicans in Florida (which I have), I might want to interview someone whose passion is Florida seabirds (which I did). Doing a little research will impress your readers, and it will lend your story some authority.

FIND YOUR FOCUS

39. Decide what your essay is about. Let's say the prompt asks you to choose an important learning moment from your high school days. That's a good prompt, but if you choose it, you are only choosing a topic, and topics tend to be broad. One useful trick is to narrow the topic as much as you can — not to a semester in your literature course, but that day you had an argument with your teacher about whether to honor a great poem that was written by a notorious person.

40. Decide what your essay is REALLY about. At Poynter when we give an easy writing prompt, such as "Describe your favorite dessert," we ask the writers two questions: What is your story about? Imagine your answer is "powdered donuts." Then we might ask, what is your story REALLY about? That's when we get to go deeper. Perhaps you have a powerful memory of your first crush buying you a powdered donut on a school field trip. Perhaps your mom and dad loved powdered donuts and eating them feels like carrying on a family tradition. The key is to ask yourself the two questions.

41. Choose a focus that will allow you to show and tell. Remember that focus is the central act of the writing process: learning, as you write, the heart of what you are trying to communicate about yourself and the world. Emme Slaughter understood clearly what her focus was: She had overcome obstacles often placed in front of women who aspire to become scientists. She tells us this in plain language and also shows it to us so we can experience her frustrations within her family, and her triumphs, as she raises a trophy she earned at science camp.

42. Start thinking about a title. Whether or not you are asked to include a title with your essay, I would recommend brainstorming titles and including one you think is worthy. A strong title is another way of expressing your focus, of capturing the attention of the reader, and perhaps playing with language in an interesting way. As I was first writing this, my editors and I had not yet chosen a title for this book. My working title was *Write Your Way In*, the idea being that a good essay can help get you into college, grad school, or law school. Later in life, strong writing skills might help you get a job, promotion, or grant. Even if the publisher chooses something else (and they did!), that working title has helped me keep my eyes on the prize.

43. Choose a focus that will let you begin with a bang. We have covered the importance of the lead paragraph to your essay. It is important to add that a strong lead should capture the focus of your story. It may be an anecdote, a small story that reveals your passion for science, or math, or literature. It may be a statement that expresses your big idea, or it may hint at that big idea to come.

44. Make a list of the things you want readers to know about you. I love lists, and I often write lists that do not appear in my essay as lists. I just wrote a Facebook post about my twelve favorite Christmas songs, and it appeared as a list.

But that list could then help me write a full essay about holi-day music in the rock and roll era. If I were writing my col-lege essay now, I would make a list of values and virtues that I want to attach to my own experience. I would want to prove, for example, that I am well-read, clever with language, pas-sionate about the writing and the reading of stories. Now I must show the evidence.

45. Choose a focus that is brainy, but not obnoxiously so. The fact is that in certain matters — let's say physics or calculus — you may be brainier than your reader. If you are passionate about economics, you might want to avoid focus-ing on an obscure macroeconomic theorem and instead choose a focus that allows you to describe an economic con-cept in everyday language: "My friend was wondering why he is paying three bucks for a gallon of gas, while his grandpa back in the day had to pay only thirty cents." I asked him: "Have you ever heard of inflation?"

46. Find a focus that reflects the things you know best, or care about the most. This is not as difficult as it might look. You are already an expert on some things — especially your own experience. You know yourself — your strengths and weaknesses — more than your parents, siblings, or teach-ers do. Your knowledge, your interests, your training, your experiences are wider and deeper than you imagine. Find that thing, that person, that interest to which you bring the most passion.

47. Focus on a topic that connects with your intended college experience. In high school, I thought I wanted to become a lawyer someday, until my guidance counselor suggested that English might be a good major. The point is, many high school students don't yet know what career — or even what major — they might want to pursue, and that's OK. If that's the case for you, your essay can reveal your general intelligence and curiosity. But if you do have a target in mind, your essay is a good place to show it. Let's say you want to be an engineer; you could write a story that lets the reader know how you always imagined building bridges when you were growing up.

SELECT THE BEST

48. Gather more than you need — a lot more. Once you've collected things that might be in your story, you need to curate what you have collected, and choose which characters, which anecdotes, which quotes, should go into your story. You might think that the fewer items you collect, the easier they will be to curate, but in fact, the opposite is true. If you need, say, three great anecdotes to put in your story, collect ten great anecdotes. That allows you to pick the best of the best.

49. Annotate your notes. When I was in high school, I was not good at taking notes. I learned that skill in college, and then working with journalists, who are furious notetakers. Today, I still like to take notes in a small notebook or on a legal pad, sometimes even on a napkin in a coffee shop. You may prefer to use a notes mode or app on your phone.

Regardless of what you use, let's say you have twice as much stuff in your notes than there is room for in your essay. Begin to mark up your notes. I put a star next to a quote I know I want to use. In the margin, I might add a comment: "Could be my first quote."

50. Opt for evidence over repetition. If you know what the focus of your essay is, you want to reinforce it while avoiding unnecessary repetition. To do so, it's not enough to vary how you articulate your focus: You must vary the evidence. Put the focus in your lead, follow it up with a quote, introduce an anecdote, and then summarize it at the end. All those elements will support your focus without feeling repetitive.

51. Look for details that appeal to the senses. As a reader, I love it when the writer introduces details about food. At its best, food writing offers an experience that can make your mouth water. In my personal essays, I have written about the texture of tapioca pudding on my tongue. I have written about the smell of pink bubble gum in a pack of baseball cards. But writing about food isn't the only way to appeal to the senses. I have also written about the sound of my daughter playing Santa in a kindergarten play, and how her ho-ho-ho made everyone laugh. A writer's first instinct is usually to capture the visual, but the other senses need attention, too.

52. Name things. Too many names in a short essay may be distracting. But if you are writing about the three dogs you rescued one day along the side of a busy interstate, by all means include their eventual names — Olive, Rosie, and Dakota — in your account. When you know the name of something, it reveals something about your personality. I know, for example, that the official bird of Florida is not the flamingo, but the mockingbird. That the brown pelican, the official bird of St. Pete, is different from the white pelican. Did a bird fly into your house the other day? Did it take you two hours to get it out safely? Do your best to find out the type of bird.

53. Look for potential backup singers. Many star vocalists hire backup singers to enrich the sound. It's the same with writers. You are the lead singer, but who do you want singing behind you? You can introduce a backup singer — whether Mozart, Marilyn Monroe, or a member of your family — by alluding to them. Or you can quote something that they have said that harmonizes with your story.

54. Reveal well-roundedness. Depending upon your focus and your personal writing voice, you can choose backup singers from high culture (philosophy, history, literature, etc.) or popular culture (movies, memes, music, etc.) or both. For example, I might mention that the Greek philosopher Plato wanted to throw poets out of the Republic but that his student Aristotle wanted to keep them in. And in that same essay I might quote lines from a Bruce Springsteen song, or joke about the phrase "yada, yada," which I learned from *Seinfeld*, a television sitcom. A wide range of cultural references demonstrates your well-roundedness.

BUILD A STRUCTURE

55. Read a variety of student essays to see how they are constructed. In this book and in others, you can find examples of good student essays. I recommend reading these to see how they are constructed. It's like what you would do if you wanted to become a chef. You'd need a recipe, of course. But you would also want to see what a wonderful version of that dish looks like with all the ingredients put together, and then taste it. When you read, see if you can identify the ingredients, just as you would in a dish.

56. Read essays of different lengths. I once wrote an essay for the *New York Times*. On its website, it was 1,200 words. The printed paper cut it down to eight hundred words. For a blog, it was three hundred words, and then fewer for social networks. All from the same material. You may be asked by different schools to write to different lengths. You can get a feel for how those work through your reading. Here is the key: The shorter the essay, the more work each word must do.

57. Identify your beginning, middle, and end. Every building, whether it is small or large, has a roof, a structure, and a foundation. Similarly, whether your essay is short or long, it needs a beginning, a middle, and an end. Sort through the material you have collected and mark where in the essay each particular element might go. Let's say you have selected twelve elements to go into your essay. Write each on an index card or sticky note and designate where in your story it is most likely to fit: beginning, middle, or end. Put the cards or notes in order.

58. Work from a simple plan. It has been years since I have written a formal outline for a story or even a book. Instead, I work from a list. That list contains the five or ten elements that I imagine will go into the story. I study the list. I play with it. I might try to order the elements from one to ten, but if I can't do that, I at least try to choose the one element where I can begin writing, and then build from there.

59. Look out for the lead. We sometimes talk about research (or reporting) and writing as if they were two different things. They come together not just on the practice page, but, more significantly, in your brain. I once went out as a reporter on a police call and wrote: "A 127-pound boy helped lift a 2,000-pound car off a 347-pound man." It was one of those stories about how in an emergency adrenaline fuels the body to do remarkable things. As I was gathering those facts, the idea for that opening popped in my head, which made the rest easy to write.

60. Use the middle to "raise the stakes." I love this move in storytelling, for both fiction and nonfiction. A problem is introduced at the beginning of a story, and as the character is trying to solve it, they encounter an obstacle in the middle. The essays in this book illustrate this on numerous occasions. In Emme Slaughter's essay, for example, we learn that she is mocked by boys in her family for winning the football pool. But she does not want to be a professional gambler. The stakes are raised when she recognizes the sexist obstacles in front of her as she aspires to become an astrophysicist. Remember the student with the broken necklace with a cross? The story takes a great emotional move when we find the roadside cross that marks where her father was murdered.

61. Reward the reader with a kicker of an ending. I have read a lot of stories and essays that trail off at the end. Far more satisfying are the clever endings known as kickers. No one is exactly sure where that word came from. My favorite theory is that dancers onstage — such as the Rockettes — would end their performance with a synchronized kick line. Regardless, a kicker makes readers glad they read the story to the end. It also makes not just the ending, but the entire story, more memorable.

62. Remember that nothing is set in stone. We have yet to get to the part of the process known as revision, but it will help you to know that revision is more than correcting your mistakes or changing a word or two. *Revise* literally means "to see again." You can revise everything. You can add more examples in the middle, or take some out. You can take the beginning and swap it with the end — and then change your mind again. With each change, you can ask yourself, "What will happen if I change this? What will it do for the reader's experience?"

WRITE YOUR DRAFT

63. Get into the habit of scribbling whenever you can. The more you write, the easier it gets. I can think of no writing assignment, at any level from student to professional, where it is counterproductive to get your hands moving. I've heard that novelist Lauren Groff once banged out a draft of a novel using a poetic form, and then threw it away, and sat down and began the prose version. Write what you want. When you want. But write.

64. Start writing earlier than you think you can. Don't wait until all the elements are perfectly in place. This happens all the time in the world of journalism and in scholarly work. The writer does weeks, months, years of research: so much front-end work that deadlines approach like thunderstorms. A common excuse for not writing is "I still don't know enough. I have to do more research." When I find a writer in that state, I might say to them, "Put all your notes and research aside. Please sit down for an hour and start writing. If it helps, put 'Dear Roy' at the top, as if you were sending me a message about your story." Here is what happens when you write earlier than you think you can: (1) You learn what you already know, and (2) you learn what you still need to learn. It will make your process more efficient.

65. Bang out a zero draft. Many writers, including some famous ones, hate their early drafts. I don't know why. I love my early drafts because they are the first expression of what I want to say. I love the term "zero draft" because it will be written so quickly that it won't even look like a first draft. When you write a zero draft, you don't have to care yet about accuracy, about spelling and technical aspects of grammar and usage, about a smooth and readable style. You only need to care about getting ideas on a page — fast.

66. Remember that no one cares what your first draft looks like. In high school, I was chosen as salutatorian of the class of 1966 (the Beatles were popular!), which meant I had to write a brief speech and deliver it before an audience of family, friends, and about a thousand strangers. I wrote a draft and read it to one of my English teachers, John Kane. He gave a forthright critique, arguing that the speech was too general, that it lacked language that people could see and feel. I revised the speech, memorized it (not necessary), and had a successful delivery. That was more than a half-century ago. Some classmates still remember that day, but not a single one of them knows that I had an imperfect first draft. In fact, close readers will be impressed when they know that you turned a flimsy first draft into something memorable.

67. Draft your essay in your head. Imagine how it will look on the page or the screen, how long it will be, where you will start and where you will finish, the quote that will make readers laugh or think or cry.

68. Put your notes aside. One of America's most honored writers is John McPhee, author of long stories that appear in *The New Yorker* magazine, narratives that have been turned into many popular nonfiction books. He testifies that he is a scrupulous notetaker with a very systematic process. But once he gets his material organized, he says that he just sits at the keyboard and starts writing, without referring to his notes. That helps him conjure up his most important memories, his most compelling scenes, the best stuff that bubbles to the top of his mind. You can do that, too.

69. Take us on a journey. A story, remember, is an experience you give the reader, not an inventory of facts, not a list of your honors, not your résumé. One great way to build a draft of a story is to think chronologically. Something happens: You drive your car into a snowy ditch on Christmas Eve. That would be a good inciting incident. But readers will want to know what happens next. And what happens after that, and that, and that? Where will we end up? Think of a story as a form of transportation, even a time machine, allowing readers to travel into the past, perhaps to a time before they were born, to a place they have never visited.

REVISION MEANS "TO SEE AGAIN"

70. Revision is not just proofreading to find errors. It is important to check your work to find as many mistakes as possible. But revision is much more than that. For some writers it means putting the first draft aside and starting again. For others it means cutting 2,000 words down to 750 words. The key is to begin drafting early enough so that you have time to make the important changes that will show off your best work.

71. You can revise at every step in the process: the idea, the research, the focus, the structure, the draft; and you can revise a revision. If your story or essay is not working for you, it often means that one part of the process has broken down. You can turn the dial backward to find a source of the problem. Does the draft have a good structure? Have you selected the best material to include? Do you have a sharp focus, or are you drifting here and there? Have you done enough reporting on your own experience in order to gather wonderful stuff? Is your idea interesting enough? Did you pick the best prompt? In revision, every section, paragraph, sentence, and word is up for grabs, a candidate for change.

72. Read it aloud to yourself — and then to others. Not all writers read their work aloud, but many do for many reasons. Does the work sound like me? Does it present the best version I have to offer, one that will attract my important readers? We read with our eyes, of course, but we also read with our ears. Something that looks good on the page or screen may not sound good. Sometimes I imagine that I am writing for the best versions of public radio, the stories that are filled with drama, or the reports that make hard facts easy listening. Don't read it aloud right away. Let it cool off for a while. Then come back to the text with fresh eyes — and ears — and read it aloud. You will become more confident about the elements that work, and better able to spot the ones that need more attention.

73. Start sentences with subjects and verbs. Some of the strongest sentences are structured thus: subject (what the sentence is about) + verb (the action or status of the subject) + object (the receiver of the action). It is as easy as 1-2-3: "Maria lost her grandmother's ring." There are a thousand variations, but here's the most important thing to look for during revision: Make sure that your subjects and verbs are not separated by so many other words that the reader loses track of who did what.

74. End sentences with a bang. Check to see if you have placed important words at the ends of sentences, especially at the end of paragraphs. This is so important that it is worth repeating. Finding the right words is good. Placing them in the right order is better. The period is a stop sign. Any word or phrase that sits right before the stop sign gets special emphasis.

75. Don't hide important elements in the middle of sentences or paragraphs. Remember when I wrote the sentence "The Queen is dead, my lord." I was hiding the most important word, *dead*, in the middle. When I took the word out of hiding, I began writing as Shakespeare does in *Macbeth*: "The Queen, my lord, is dead."

76. Vary the length of sentences to create a pleasant rhythm. If I want to make something clear, I use shorter sentences. But an essay made up entirely of short sentences sounds dull, and I don't want my readers to fall asleep. Instead, I vary sentence length. Some sentences have twenty words, others only three. Check out the length of my sentences in this paragraph: 10, 11, 20, 5, 8, 16. All relatively short, but the variation creates what I hope is a nice rhythm.

77. Express your best idea in a short sentence. This is an old trick and an important one. As you revise your work, see if you can find a sentence, or maybe a paragraph, that contains your most important idea. For Emme Slaughter, it was a message to boys and men who might ridicule or resent her interest in science: "Get used to it." Four one-syllable words. If you can't find such a sentence in your essay, get a pencil and paper and write me an imaginary answer to this request: Please tell me the most important thing this essay says about you — in ten words or fewer. For this book, mine might be: "Write the story only you can write." Or "Don't try to deny it: You are a writer." Or "The good writer is the honest writer."

AVOID PITFALLS

78. Always be honest. Don't rip off another writer, including any in this book. The tools in this book are not tools to help you steal. They are tools for originality. All writers borrow from other writers. But if you do, make sure you give credit, especially if you are using language that is distinctive. Sometimes you use a phrase that you know is not original, but you don't know who to attribute the phrase to. When I can't find the answer on Google, I write around that problem this way: "Whoever described the internet as an 'information superhighway' has probably now discovered that it's more like a polluted ocean, with a few treasures buried at the bottom."

79. Don't make up events that did not happen. If plagiarism is the first big literary no-no, fabrication is the second. If you had a conversation with your French granny in Montreal, please don't write that it happened in Paris, at the Louvre, in view of the *Mona Lisa*. Such changes turn a truthful essay into fiction. That said, you can do just about anything if you let your readers in on it. For example, you might say, "We were sitting at Granny's kitchen table in Montreal when she told me the story of the day she left her childhood home in France, but I like to imagine that it happened in Paris, at the Louvre, in view of the *Mona Lisa*." No one expects you to remember everything that happened years ago perfectly. But you know when you are intentionally making stuff up. It's not ethical, and you risk sounding phony. Please, don't do it.

80. Avoid gimmicks. In the movie *Legally Blonde*, Reese Witherspoon's character gets accepted into Harvard Law School with a personal statement written on pink stationery and a poolside video in which she is wearing a skimpy bikini. That is satire. Devote all your creative energy to making your essay compelling. You don't want to distract the reader with any gimmicks. They might set your work apart in ways you don't intend.

81. Do not pay someone to write it for you. When I was in graduate school, I met an old high school friend who was in summer school and struggling to write a paper. He was panicked, and I felt sorry for him, so I wrote the essay for him. Later he gave me $50. We didn't get caught, but we easily could have. This confession is to caution you against buying an essay, either from an unscrupulous company or from an individual who may be a more skillful writer than you are. You've probably heard news stories about the "Varsity Blues" scandal in which rich and famous parents, some of them Hollywood stars, paid off people at prestigious colleges to admit their kids. As of this writing, thirty-eight parents have pleaded guilty or have been convicted of crimes, and at least thirty have gone to prison.

82. Do not use text provided by chatbots. If someone reads this book fifty years from now, who knows, maybe robots will have taken over the world. That's what happens in the movies, right? If you are doing some research for your essay, I see no problem in using AI tools such as ChatGPT. It can search the internet at high speeds. But in 2024, the bots produce writing that is inelegant, with information that is often inaccurate. More important, passing this writing off as your own is a form of cheating — one that colleges are getting better and better at detecting.

83. If a parent volunteers to write it for you, say NO. Your parents and other family members can be very helpful to you as you think through how to tell your story. But, in the end, it is YOUR story and not theirs. Look at tip #91 to see how parents can provide the best, most honest help.

84. Avoid tired topics. I have been told by readers in the admissions office that there are certain topics they see all the time. This does not surprise me. After all, the writers are following the same prompts. One reader told me he had read too many stories about dead grandparents, divorced parents, or "the day I met a poor person." The value of brainstorming for several prompts is that you will find that essay that only you can write.

85. Be careful with sensitive or polarizing topics. However experienced and professional your readers are, they bring their own biases to the act of reading and may have a strong negative reaction to a controversial topic. Perhaps you had an abortion. Or you bought a handgun with your own money. Or you are growing marijuana in your backyard. Or you think that people who are different from you have been given an unfair advantage. Race, ethnicity, gender, and how you choose to identify yourself can be fruitful topics for your writing efforts. But the edgier your approach, the better it is to test the work with a variety of readers before you submit it.

HOW TO GET HELP

86. Don't be embarrassed to ask for help. Knowing how to get the help you need is a lifetime skill, from the cradle to the grave. If you are struggling with your essay, there is no shame in asking for the help you need.

87. Find out whether your school offers classes or resources. If you are lucky, your school may teach classes or lessons on the craft of the personal essay. They may offer guidance through workshops. Ask your favorite teacher or a school counselor what resources are available to you.

88. Seek tutoring outside of school. (But be careful.) My daughter Lauren is a language and math tutor at St. Petersburg College, so I know how effective tutors can be. And Michelle Hiskey is a veteran writer who has tutored many students — at a variety of skill levels — on their personal essays. There are many businesses that offer all kinds of tutoring in all aspects of getting into college. A good book may cost $25. A professional tutoring service may cost many times that amount. If you are seeking such a service, be sure to check on financial aid opportunities.

89. Turn to videos, podcasts, and books. The books I have read on the topic of college essays were written more than a decade ago, before the pandemic, before Supreme Court rulings on affirmative action, before the onslaught of artificial intelligence. Some have been updated. All of them contain some useful advice. Be sure to search for free videos and podcasts. They are not for everyone, but maybe you will find one that is just right for your needs.

90. Work with a writing coach. I know a lot about coaching writers of all ages, and as an author I know how to work with editors who have coached me through big projects, including this one. Here are some tips: Find an encouraging coach who can guide you throughout the process, from the idea stage all the way to revision. This can be a paid coach, or someone in your life who is invested in your future. The coach should NOT rewrite your drafts. The coach should ask you open-ended questions that lead you to good decisions: What prompt do you think will generate your best essay?

Have you found a focus? What do you want readers to think about you after they read your work? I know you are just starting your essay, but have you thought of an ending yet?

91. Coach your parents to coach you. Parents can be your best helpers, or they can drive you crazy. As a parent, I have done both for/to my daughters. If your parents want to be involved, they can help you remember things you want to write about. They can offer encouragement and gentle reminders that you should get back to work. But you might not want to share early drafts of the story with your parents, at least until you have gotten some reaction from other sources (readers, teachers, friends). It was hard for me as a parent not to "take control" of my daughters' writing, to seize a text and start scribbling corrections. You're lucky if they want to help. Like good coaches, they will help you most by asking you questions. It's your job to figure out what works and what needs more work.

92. Use digital resources. By now you will have learned the benefits, personal and academic, and also the dangers of online resources like ChatGPT. The best learning resource I had in my high school days was probably a multivolume encyclopedia such as the World Book. Now I can reach into my pocket and search for knowledge about topics both trivial and serious. There's nothing wrong with using search engines and other sources to gain background information and detail about the topic you are working on: What is the name of the oldest living tortoise? Who was Marie Curie and how did she become the first woman to win a Nobel Prize? How long is this trail I just hiked in Appalachia? Warning: Check with helpers to make sure a site is reliable, not a source of misinformation. Double-check important details.

93. Get help in checking spelling, grammar, and usage. In my writing world, the world of this book, I get a lot (not *alot*!) of proofreading help from many capable people. I have a wonderful agent who reads my work. I have at least two editors reading my manuscript, marking up things I must pay attention to. Then we send it to the copy editors, who correct my mistakes, including some factual errors, and make suggestions on how to strengthen my sentences. A proofreader gets a final read (until I read it again). Even with all that help, mistakes sneak into my book to be corrected in future editions. If you are wondering if it is OK for you to get help checking your work, down to the commas and periods, the answer is yes, yes, yes. This careful checking need not come early in the process, but it must come eventually if you are to give yourself the best chance of submitting an error-free essay.

94. Fact-check yourself. You may have gotten help from a teacher, a writing coach, a parent, a digital grammar checker, a tutor, a counselor, a church helper, an older sibling, even some fellow students who know more about the technical aspects of language. But it's your job to check the facts and details in the writing. Print out a draft of your essay and check every name and detail. Reporters I know do a final reading and a double check. If it checks out, what do they put in the margin? A check mark of course. ✓

95. Pat yourself on the back. You have done the work. You have joined the club of readers and writers. As a student, I knew early on I was a member of the club. I loved reading stories — even long grown-up novels — and I had fun writing, usually humor or satire. Over time it became part of my identity: I had the power to tell stories that revealed my true self and helped give meaning to others. If you have read this book, if you have done your best to write an authentic personal essay, you have won the right to call yourself a writer, now and for the rest of your life. Welcome to the club.

TAKE ACTION TO HELP OTHERS

96. Advocate for good writing in your school and community. Start a writers' group, either for your personal essay or for other writing projects.

97. Hang out in independent book stores. If you lived in St. Petersburg, Florida, I would take you to Tombolo Books. There you would find not only wonderful texts, but also topics that could turn into essays — such as the importance of reading banned books.

98. Instead of giving an apple to your favorite English or writing teacher, share a copy of this book. Invite the teacher and other students to engage in conversations about the best student essays. You can begin by discussing your favorite essays in this book and why they work for you.

99. Mentor younger writers. If you have written your

essay and been accepted into the school of your choice, and you feel confident enough, start a team of senior writers willing to help younger students develop good topics for their essays.

AND...

100. Keep writing. Your college essay is not the last important assignment you will ever have to write. Far from it! My final wish for you is that you take the advice in this book and carry it into the college of your choice, or wherever you land. When you do, use the advice for some of your other writing assignments. Knowing something about the writing process, understanding how stories work, feeling the power of your authentic voice on the page or on the screen — these are rockets that can launch you into a successful academic career. Cheers.

PART IX

The Power of Revision

From this section you can learn:

* The differences between revision and proofreading
* Strategies for taking a good essay and making it better
* The ability to recognize what works in your essay and what needs work
* How questions from a coach, or questions you ask yourself about a draft, can lead to something better

FROM FIRST DRAFT TO FINAL

In writing, there is a Now, but also a Before and an After. The Before is created by the writer in the form of a rough early draft. It does not matter how rough it is because there will be an After. That better draft will be the result of revision, and, if you are lucky, the changes you make will be the result of consultation with a reliable writing coach. I have played that role with students for almost fifty years. If you have no access to a coach, worry not. The tools you learn here will help you coach yourself, as when you ask yourself "What is this story really about?"

Michelle Hiskey is one of Atlanta's best feature writers, who, after working at Emory University, began coaching students on how to write their college essays. She will be describing for us her coaching method. With the generosity of her students, she will also be sharing essays that she helped writers revise. Remember that revision, at its best, is not just about scratching out a few words or checking the spelling. That's proofreading. Good coaching leads writers to revision of the big parts of the process: the shaping of ideas, the collection of details, the articulation of a focus, selection of the most relevant and interesting items, construction of a coherent structure, building a draft, and working hard to clarify and perfect it.

You are about to read the work of six high school writers whose work was improved by collaborating with Michelle.

You will find a first draft, Michelle's analysis of its strengths and weaknesses, and the revision. After each case study you will find the most important coaching lesson.

CASE STUDIES: BEFORE AND AFTER

Case #1
Natural Hair

By Alina Heredia
(accepted to Smith College)

Early Draft

(635 words)

I saw a cloud of smoke coming from my hair, pain seared through my scalp and neck. My body jolted forward and filled with goosebumps.

"Ow it burns," I exclaimed.

"Stop moving," my mom said.

"But it hurts!"

"Well you want pretty hair, right?"

Growing up my mom permed my hair to kill my natural curls. In Dominican culture big curly hair is seen as ugly and disorderly. I never saw what my natural hair looked like growing up and have no memory of what it looked like. Whenever I complained of the pain she always responded "well you want pretty hair, right?"

I thought I did, straight hair was all I knew, I thought I looked pretty with straight hair. To some extent I was willing to endure pain, burns, and harsh hair pulling. Just like in life we are willing to endure pain and hardships because we enjoy the end result. My end result was beauty. I wanted to be beautiful.

Sitting down in that chair I was alone with my thoughts. I questioned whether this pain was worth the outcome. Why did I have to go through pain to be beautiful? I made a promise to myself that when I get older and had full control of my hair I wouldn't put myself through this pain. I would buy my own products and do my hair how I wanted to.

When that time had come it wasn't what my younger self had anticipated. I constantly straightened my hair, it became a routine. Every other week I was at the salon damaging my natural hair. I had sunken myself into a deeper hole. As much as I wanted to stop I couldn't.

I loathed how big my hair was. It was overwhelming, my face drowned under all my hair. The layers of my tightly coily hair were too difficult to maintain and style. My classmates always told me that I looked better with straight hair, after hearing it so many times I started believing it. I wanted to please other people and in doing so I also didn't want to spend hours trying to style my hair. It was a win-win situation, or so I thought.

With trial and error, it took time to feel confident in my natural hair. When I finally did, I remember I got ready to leave my house and before I did my sister stopped me and stroked my hair saying, "oh my god! I love your hair, it's so big." I strutted the streets with the utmost confidence. There wasn't an ounce of doubt in my mind. I was complimented by strangers on my hair. It was like a breath of fresh air.

I learned that all along I just needed to be proud of my hair and it looks like and wear it confidently. It took a long time for me to love my hair in its natural state because of years of believing "good" and "pretty" hair meant straight hair. I was also just about embracing my blackness which something I wasn't taught to do growing up. Realizing this my hair, this is what it does, this is what it looks like, and that's okay. My hair is beautiful and it's me and I don't need to change it or tame it to fit any body or society's standards on what pretty hair is. A huge issue in society, where girls with big curly hair are told to tame their hair and straighten it because it's too big, wild, it looks unkempt, or it's unprofessional. I am told I look prettier when I straighten my hair, making me hate the hair that grows from my head. Once I stopped trying to conform to what society deems beautiful, I was free to be my authentic self.

Analysis by coach Michelle Hiskey

It was a pleasure to coach Alina on her story about her hair. Everyone has a hair story (or a no-hair story), but this writer offers so much more. Her first draft begins with a kind of dramatic action, one that draws the reader into the story. She begins:

> I saw a cloud of smoke coming from my hair, pain seared through my scalp and neck. My body jolted forward and filled with goosebumps.

It turns out that in her culture, straight hair is often preferred to big and curly, and our writer is trapped between belonging to a cherished heritage and wanting to be an independent player.

My job as coach is to see the strengths in an essay, but also to see the unfulfilled potential. The writer's initial draft invites us into the "small universe" of hair as a marker of beauty and acceptance in her family and culture. Revising an essay to go from good to great takes a lot more work than going from average to better. It requires the writer to refine and specify. Yes, it's a story about hair, but hair carries the bigger struggle: What does it mean for the writer to be herself in this family and this kind of culture at this exact time in history? Sometimes I call these mirror essays, because the writer is using something—in this case, hair—as a mirror that reflects who they are.

In most personal essays, your solution is your story. The initial draft of this story presented a complex issue of caring for this particular type of hair, but the solution was not described in similar depth. It needed more balance. When I asked the writer how she got up to speed on caring for natural hair, she described specific steps of gaining that knowledge. You'll see these details in the revision, and it is a vivid picture of what her optimal hair solution required of her.

A big part of essay writing that many writers miss, surprisingly and to their major detriment, is examining their critical moments of personal choice. In life, sometimes we are not aware that we are even making a choice or have one. But even not making a choice is a choice, and every choice will reveal your thinking and values in that moment. When you took a decisive action, what else might you have chosen instead? When this writer said she "couldn't stop" treating her hair in the way that her mother had, I asked her for more explanation. She had the power to choose, so what inside her kept her from changing? This led to a clearer understanding that her hair was a way of proving that she belonged, that she was accepted, that she was beautiful in the eyes of others.

Another very important question to ask about a narrative essay like this, which involves personal transformation: Can you briefly describe a time when your new thinking was tested? This question led to a new anecdote about a relative who criticized the writer's hair and in which the writer's reaction shows her new mindset. See how much more powerful this essay is with that change. When you show how you've changed, you own the change.

Revised Draft

(642 words)

I saw a cloud of smoke from the corner of my eye as pain seared through my scalp and neck. I smelled the pungent odor of burning hair. My body jolted forward and filled with goosebumps.

"Ow! It burns," I exclaimed.

"Stop moving," Mami said.

"But it hurts!"

Growing up, my mom permed my hair to kill my natural curls. In Dominican culture, big curly hair is seen as ugly and disorderly. Whenever I complained of the pain, she always responded, "Well, you want pretty hair, right?"

I agreed that I looked pretty with straight hair and was inclined to make sacrifices for it. I so desperately wanted acceptance, wanted everyone to see I was well put together—even if that meant sitting in a chair for endless hours tolerating harsh hair-pulling and burns. I was sacrificing my natural hair and identity for the approval of others, because I in my raw and natural form wasn't enough.

Sitting down in that chair, I began to question why I had to go through pain to be beautiful. I promised myself that when I got to middle school and had full control of my hair, I wouldn't put myself through this pain. I would buy my own products and do my hair how I wanted.

When that time came, that wasn't what happened. I kept the routine of straightening my hair. Instead of my mom doing it, every other week I was at the salon damaging my natural hair. My classmates always told me that I looked better with straight hair, and after hearing it so many times, I believed it. I still wanted to please other people and not spend hours trying to style my hair. I had sunk into a deeper hole, believing that I had to do all of this to be worthy.

As much as I wanted to stop, I could not. I had no clue how to, and it seemed nearly impossible. My natural hair was overwhelming and my face drowned under all of it. The layers of my tight, coily hair needed specific products, careful combing, and a good cut to even have a chance at looking good.

Even though I loathed how big my natural hair was, I wanted to learn how to love and care for it, but I didn't know where to start. My oldest sister had always defiantly worn her hair out curly, so naturally, I turned to her for help.

With her guidance, my own trial and error, numerous

YouTube videos, endless products, and trips to salons that specialize in natural hair, finding my natural beauty finally seemed possible. I almost gave up a few times because I hated to wear my hair out, but I learned to love my hair in every form.

One day before I left my house, my sister stopped me and stroked my hair. "Oh my god!" she said. "I love your hair, it's so big." That day I strutted the streets with the utmost confidence. I was complimented by strangers. It was like a breath of fresh air; my natural hair had never received so much appreciation before.

Then one afternoon my mom's cousin came over. From the corner of my eye, I saw him approaching. I felt fingers brushing the surface of my hair and then a gentle grasp at my roots.

"What is it with young girls these days wearing their hair out looking all crazy like this? Is this a new trend?" he said.

I didn't bother to respond or engage. I removed myself from his grasp and walked to the other side of the room. I shrugged off his remark because people are always going to judge. But my judgment of my hair and my identity is what matters.

There isn't an ounce of doubt in my mind, my natural hair is beautiful.

Key coaching lesson: In the revision the writer shows — not just tells — her personal transformation of learning to love

her hair. She adds small details about her sister helping her style her hair, and she uses words and images that appeal to the senses. She finds her mirror in other people appreciating her hair.

Case #2
Two Cultures Drawn by Hand

By Jordi Schuler
(accepted to Dickinson College)

Early draft

(944 words)

Sad stories about Cuba again?? I would sigh to myself every time we went to visit my Abuela and Abu. They seemed otherworldly. So different from everyone else I knew. They were a source of embarrassment. I hated the barrage of Spanish spoken too fast. I hated the smell of the Cuban cigars my Abu and his friends would smoke after dinner while they told stories in Spanish that I could not follow. Abuela's food seemed strange and not like what I saw in my white elementary school cafeteria. Nobody was pulling arroz con picadillo out of their lunchbox.

I felt the least Cuban or Spanish when I was around my Cuban and Spanish grandparents. With my friends from school, I felt like I was not white and all-American enough. I felt divided and resentful in having to participate in family things because it all felt forced onto me. I wanted to be doing anything else but embracing my heritage in my free time. I now know this isolating feeling is very commonly felt by kids born of two cultures.

In a family where even my white father spoke Spanish, I felt like the black sheep for not pursuing it as much as my sister did. I grew up feeling very different from my family—they are all introverted while I am more extroverted. Because we didn't always see eye to eye, I developed a lot of methods to cope with my confusing feelings.

One major way I could organize my thoughts was my journaling through sketchbooks. Writing didn't appeal to me as much as doodling to get my feelings on the page and help me better interpret what was going on in my life. "Doodling" something has a negative connotation, like it's not serious enough. But these insignificant little drawings had a big impact on my mental health and who I have become.

My doodles are spread out within the pages of three black National Gallery of Art sketchbooks. They are sequential and, much like a diary, I would write the date so that I could look back and see the progression of my thoughts and feelings as well as art style. To anyone but me, they might look like scribbles or an incoherent grouping of dissimilar ideas and images. Yet the pages organized by day would be the mirror I held up to my daily experience to reflect on what I was feeling.

I would always use a black pen for line work and because I like the simple elegance of black and white together. When I would use color, which was rare, I would use nonconventional materials like crayons or chalk to add emphasis to an idea or a portion of my day.

I now know that this was a way to compartmentalize and examine my feelings of not belonging.

Recently I met someone new at school who feels like a mirror of my past self. In some ways, we are nothing alike. Renzo is a 15-year-old from Peru. He has only been in the US for three weeks. He barely speaks English.

Rico and I immediately hit it off, as he feels like a fish out of water in this new country and I in many ways have felt that same way before. In a class where our phones are taken up, we were unable to use Google Translate, so we had to get creative. We were immediately able to communicate through doodles and my limited Spanish / his limited English. Our connecting felt like a real full circle moment since I was able to use this talent that I have depended on for so long and my Spanish, which I once actively did not want to learn. It's been nice for him to be able to practice English and meet new people and the opposite has been true for me. I now know there are valuable connections I would have never been able to make without embracing my Latin heritage.

With age has come an appreciation of my grandparents' sacrifices and what they had to overcome to immigrate to three different countries and set up a life in each one. They are different from everyone else I know and I could not be more thankful for that. My Abuela has taught me to hold on to memories and mementos and to not be wasteful because you never know what is ahead. My Abu has taught me about work ethic and perseverance; he's still working every day at age 80 and refuses to stop while he can be helpful to even one single person. Now I understand the barrage of Spanish and can add the occasional joke or comment. I enjoy the aroma of cigars and it reminds me of spending time with my grandfather and tios. I get a sense of satisfaction that I get to pull flavorful dishes such as arroz con picadillo out of my lunchbox.

I no longer feel passive or resistant to my Cuban and Spanish heritage. And my outlook has broadened to include all Latino cultures in the US. I actively seek out Spanish-speaking friends, music, and new experiences (including food!). One thing I am looking forward to in college is joining cultural affinity groups, such as Black Student Union and Latin American/Latino Student Association, and learning much more about Latin

American and US Latino History and customs. I am
actively searching for ways to dedicate myself to
inclusive community building.

I now know that my dual heritage uniquely positions
me to be a connector and interpreter between people.
This will be the daily work of my life and I look forward
to it.

Analysis by coach Michelle

In this essay, the writer, a young Cuban American, finds
himself torn between two cultures. He describes moments of
alienation when he feels like a stranger in both worlds. He
needs a creative outlet, and he finds it in the visual arts, in
this case, the exquisite art of doodling.

Like Alina, Jordi is straddling two cultures. His resis-
tance to his Cuban heritage creates a kind of friction: He's
taking the reader into a place that isn't familiar or comfortable. That's where growth happens.

Many essays, including this one, fit naturally into a three-
part character arc. This writer starts with (1) resentment,
then moves into (2) acceptance, and finally discovers (3) celebration. It can be hard for writers to see this structure when
they're at the starting line, however!

Often, though, the arc of story will get lost in details that
are not necessary to capture the essay's focus. Revision is
where the writer has to let go of whatever is not serving the

essay; that way, what remains can really shine. Easier said than done. Yes, it's like sculpting a block of marble; you must keep chipping away. In Jordi's case, that meant cutting almost three hundred words.

Revised Draft

(636 words)

Sad stories about Cuba again? My Abuela and Abu were a source of embarrassment. I hated the barrage of Spanish, the earthy smell of Abu's cigars. Abuela's rich food was not what I saw in my elementary school cafeteria. Nobody was pulling arroz con picadillo out of their lunchbox.

Around my Cuban and Spanish relatives, I felt the least Cuban or Spanish. With my friends from school, I felt like I was not all-American enough. I felt divided and resentful, which I now know is an isolating feeling very commonly felt by kids born of two cultures. At home I felt like the black sheep: my parents and sister are introverts and even my white father spoke Spanish. Meanwhile, I am extroverted and avoided Spanish.

To help me better interpret what was going on in my life, I doodled in a series of National Gallery of Art sketchbooks. "Doodling" sometimes has a negative connotation, like it's not serious, but these little drawings had a big impact on who I have become. To the casual eye, they might look like scribbles or mismatched ideas and images. Yet they were the mirror I held up to my daily experience, a way to compartmentalize and examine my feelings of not belonging.

One day, I almost destroyed all this work. My mom had looked through the sketchbooks without asking and I felt so exposed, like a private part of me was on display. Maybe if I purged my creations, I would rid myself of all that made me feel different and isolated. I was beginning high school, and stifling parts of my personality to fit in at a new school. It was peak COVID, and I desperately wanted to hold on to every single person I had, even if that meant hiding the real me.

What stopped me from destroying my art and covering up my true self? That would have been untrue to who I want to be. If I lived without reflecting on the past, I would never appreciate the present and dream about the future. Not being like my peers and family means that I am my own singular person, with my own unique experiences and perspectives. To be at my best, I had to embrace all of myself.

Recently I met someone who feels like a mirror image of myself. Rico is a 15-year-old from South America who just came to the US and barely speaks English. He feels like a fish out of water, and I have certainly felt that same way. In class, without our phones and Google Translate, we immediately communicated through doodles and my limited Spanish. In that moment, I felt fully completed. I connected with and helped someone by using the drawing that I had relied on for so long and a language that I once resisted learning.

I now appreciate my grandparents' sacrifices in immigrating three times and setting up a life in each country. My Abuela has taught me to hold on to memories and mementos because you never know what is ahead and they will sustain you. My Abu is 80 and refuses to stop working while he can be helpful to even one single person, and I want to be that way too.

Now I feel satisfied whenever I pull flavorful dishes such as arroz con picadillo out of my lunchbox. I look forward to joining cultural affinity groups in college, such as the Black Student Union and Latin American / Latino Student Associations, and already I am seeking ways to dedicate myself to inclusive community building.

My drawings helped me understand who I am. I now know that my dual heritage uniquely positions me to be a connector and interpreter between people. This will be the daily work of my life, and I look forward to it.

Key coaching lesson: Many essays have no details at all, so it's great when a coach works with a writer that has lots of details. Revision helps decide which are the most important

ones: the ones central to the message or focus of the piece. Notice the details preserved in the (much shorter) revision, the one about how no other students were pulling Cuban food from their lunchboxes. Jordi keeps details about communicating with his friend Rico through doodles and parts with the details that do not help him make his point.

Case # 3
Fallacy of the Sunk Cost

By Braeden Harris
(accepted to Kennesaw State University)

Early Draft

(308 words)

Major challenges and setbacks are often the cause of major events in one's life, as without failure true success is often unattainable, Understood by influential author Dale Carnegie, "discouragement and failure are two of the surest stepping stones to success." This is acknowledged by the preponderance of athletes. Similar to other sports competitors, I climbed to reach uneven ground where setbacks became less feasible, these experiences taught me to embrace mental and physical challenges and hardships.

Moreover, coaches are hard on their athletes in order to prompt growth, however do athletes understand this? I for sure did not; setbacks and challenges are not always physical, but also mental. Throughout my course of playing baseball my enlightenment on this topic helped me grow. Rather than focusing on small mistakes, I used mental challenges to your advantage to improve. Do away with negative, irrational thinking, switch your mindset from "I missed one" to "Let's not miss another." This is where I understood that those who pushed me the hardest wanted me to grow the most.

Apart from mental setbacks and rational thinking skills, major challenges I faced in sports resulted in physical failures that I had to overcome. In my personal experience, this was elbow issues. As a slider pitcher my elbow was often overworked and 2 years into high school I heard a "snap." Ending any chance I had at further success in the sport I was pushed to find something new. This series of events led me to physical training and grew my understanding of discipline.

In conclusion, I have only been able to be as successful as I am currently due to obstacles that I have overcome in the form of failures and setbacks. Mental and physical challenges from sports have enlightened my thinking and helped me transition to a better and more successful version of myself.

Analysis by coach Michelle

Working with Braeden led to one of the most dramatic revisions I have experienced from a coaching session. The first draft was a vague, impersonal recounting of the "big sports injury" of a high school baseball pitcher.

When we met, I realized that this writer had a much keener grasp on his story than his first draft suggested. Talking out what happened to him really helped him see how remarkable his story is, not because of the big sports injury, but of how he taught himself to think differently about it and fight for himself amid a lot of family pressure.

That his insights would come not from physical therapy, but from what he learned in his AP economics class makes this not a typical hook. Fittingly, it's more like a slider pitch: a sneaky, unexpected way to frame his devastating injury and his academic/professional goals. And it works.

In revising his essay, this writer worked hard to weave in specific details and observations to create a more personal, focused essay about leaving baseball and finding his truer self. He examined the major turning points for what he might have chosen, and contrasted his truth to his parents'.

Perhaps most important, he shows not only why he left his familiar sport but also where he went next and why. His character gets stronger physically and grows psychologically in this essay. That he relies on a theory of economics is a surprising bonus and helps show him as a learner who applies big ideas to his personal life.

Revised Draft

(634 words)

The 2023 school year had just started, and day one in AP economics introduced me to the "sunk-cost fallacy" that helped me make sense of a major shift in my life. Beginning that day and throughout the class, I learned that people often invest time and money into doing something because they've done it so much. They will never consciously choose to stop doing it because they don't want to lose what they've put into it. These people keep waiting for their big return. But that's the fallacy: just because you keep doing something doesn't mean you'll get something out of it.

This learning curve spoke directly to my choice to end my baseball career in spite of the reactions of people around me. The sunk-cost fallacy helped me understand how to make the best decisions for myself, and I use it to understand how to avoid making bad decisions.

From competing on a travel team at the ripe age of 8 to committing to year-round teams in middle school, I dedicated hours to my success as a baseball pitcher. My ongoing goal was to improve, and every year I was better. For example, when I was 12, I was throwing 60 mph, but by age 14, I threw 84 mph. I also mastered off-speed pitches, and with this, I developed my slider so it curved through the strike zone so that batters couldn't hit it.

Everything was great. But sophomore year I was on the mound and when I let go of the ball, I heard a chilling snap. It was the loudest noise I had ever heard, but only I could hear it, and that was it.

After breaking my elbow, I wanted to stop playing baseball. However, my parents remained stuck within the fallacy, often making their argument that I had put so much into it. But that did not persuade me. I refused to remain helpless in a logical fallacy because it did not make sense. I saw the benefits of abandoning baseball even though my parents didn't. I knew how much I was lost and needed to find a new version of myself and dedicate myself accordingly.

I have always been a skinny kid and knew I wanted to stay healthy outside of sports, so I started working out at a gym, and that's when everything clicked again. People there were encouraging and I began to love my time there. After one year of working out, I was serious about bodybuilding, focusing on sleep and eating habits and proud of my ability to commit to something other than baseball as well as move forward from a major setback. If I had stayed with baseball just because I had so much invested in it, I would never have discovered bodybuilding.

In conclusion, I will be successful because I know that simply continuing to do something doesn't mean you'll get something out of it, and staying with what I've always done can keep me from discoveries. As I look forward to college and a business career, I know I can adapt to major issues and create solutions. While baseball taught me resilience and dedication, bodybuilding took those traits to a higher level, and I am focused around the clock on actions that develop me as a bodybuilder. I am always assessing whether I am doing something that is helping me toward a goal because I want to avoid actions that are just what I've always done without thinking. The sunk-cost fallacy has helped make me interested in economics as a college major, and I want to keep using my knowledge of logical fallacies to connect with people and make clear and concise decisions under pressure. I'm counting on these skills to guide me in college, business, and my best decisions possible.

Key coaching lesson: Don't be afraid to expand your vision to creatively connect two things that may not seem to work together. Who could guess that an economics theory would help him learn an important life lesson from the moment he heard a bone snap? The juxtaposition of two seemingly disparate elements allows the reader to understand both with greater insight.

Case #4
The Bug Club

By Evan Planeaux
(accepted to the University of Georgia)

First draft

(690 words)

Bugs have always been a part of me. They have fascinated me since I was a little boy, picking them up and examining them on the elementary school playground while the girls gossiped and boys pounded each other on the turf football field. Wielding my lunchbox as my trusty enclosure, I set off every recess with a single goal in mind, to successfully capture the most intriguing insect in the vicinity. Having limited time to explore, I aggressively turned over rocks, trudged through the thick shrubs on the periphery of the school, and weaved through the slender trees until I located an insect of my liking. Collecting my latest prize, I would quickly glance both ways, confirming that I had the eyes of no one as I swiftly slipped the critter in my lunch box.

Day in and day out I would go on these expeditions,

usually alone but occasionally accompanied by a less-interested friend. Then, one day, I found it. Just barely spotting the insect through the beads of sweat trickling down my face, it was a specimen that, at first sight, could be described as nothing short of spectacular. The insect's body was slender, possessing wings that appeared incapable of flight. Its long neck, topped by a triangular head, displayed two jet black, glassy eyes that seemingly always locked onto mine. Yet, most intriguing were its pair of intimidating claws, equipped with razor-sharp spikes.

The second I stepped off the bus, I bolted to the garage, rummaging through anything and everything that looked as though it would be hospitable for this new bug. Finally extracting a transparent bottle, I reluctantly coaxed the insect into his temporary home, before sealing the top off with some plastic wrap I had poked holes into. I peered into the bottle for hours, astonished at the insect's magnificence. Then it hit me. What was this thing? Plucking the bottle from the dusty ground and carefully sauntering towards the back door, I unlocked the door and entered the house bearing questions regarding the identity of the insect entrapped in my bottle. "It's a praying mantis," my mom said before pleading that I "get it out of the house."

This Praying Mantis became my obsession, and my fascination with it grew every time I interacted with it. Enlightening myself on its lifestyle, I discovered that these clever insects were the rulers of jungles and ecosystems all across the globe, using camouflage to blend in and snatch up any unsuspecting victims that were cursed in crossing their paths. I would scour my neighbor's backyards in hopes of finding prey, so I could experience this process for myself, and was amazed when I witnessed my very own pet praying mantis snatch and tear into a cricket that I had found beneath a rock.

Although I became very passionate about the praying mantis in particular, my fondness of other species of insects never diminished. I sought to educate my fellow classmates on the ins and outs of insects and everything that characterized them. My desire was for everyone in my class to feel the excitement that I felt whenever I spotted a black-widow spider, or a giant Luna Moth on the playground. And so I did, and created The Bug Club which talked about all the different insects you could find not only on the playground of Springdale Park Elementary school, but all over the world. Admittedly most of my classmates hardly expressed any real interest in the club, and an even smaller selected few took part in my daily recess expeditions.

But creating this Bug Club made me feel like I was influencing others and the way they felt about insects. Instead of just hearing about the insects that disgusted them, my classmates were taught about how unique and interesting insects like the Claudina butterfly were, with its brilliant blue and red colored wings. Or how fascinating the Portia jumping spider was, with its ability to use pinpoint accuracy to pounce on its helpless prey. Insects have shaped me since I was just a boy, and have fascinated me ever since. My bug hunt will never end.

Analysis by coach Michelle

The writer brings a lot of passion to the first draft of his essay, but that creates a problem: the story takes place when the writer is in elementary school, more than half his life ago. It's a charming story about a kid, maybe a future entomologist, who is crazy about insects and creates a Bug Club to spread the love. But very little is said about the years since then, and so much can happen in that span. The writer hasn't shared who he has become. I advised the writer to bring more of his present self into the story. I asked for a parallel example of his curiosity that occurred much more recently. What interest did he have now (like the one for bugs), and how did he find a way to share it (like forming the bug club)? He identified a business he had created: a monetized Instagram account for college football fans. To make room for this new content, he had to lose parts of his childhood narrative.

Perspective is an important element in a college essay. If you pick a topic that is very recent, your essay may come off as shallow. You haven't had much time to make sense of that recent interest or event, so you will need to consider connecting it to an interest or issue that you've held much longer. At the same time, if you pick a topic from a long time ago, you have to show what it means today or it will not be relevant. You want to be writing about who you are today and how you got here — that's the version of yourself that matters the most in a college essay.

This writer stood out by juxtaposing two very big worlds (bug collecting and college football) and thriving in them. This took a lot of work, but it makes for an essay that's fun to read and one the writer can be proud of.

Revised Draft

(642 words)

Bugs have fascinated me since I was a little boy. Every recess, while girls gossiped and boys pounded each other to the turf, I set off with a single goal in mind — to capture the most intriguing insect I could find. With little time to waste, I wielded my lunchbox as a trusty enclosure, turning over rocks, trudging through thick bushes, and scanning shrubbery.

Locating an insect of my liking, and glancing around to ensure no one was watching, I swiftly scooped up my latest prize for safekeeping. Then, one day, I found it: a specimen that could only be described as spectacular. At home, I peered at it for hours, astonished by its jet-black, glassy eyes, pupils that seemed perpetually locked onto mine, and huge claws covered with razor-sharp spikes. Later, I barged into the kitchen, blasting my unsuspecting mother with questions about the identity of my new discovery. "It's a praying mantis," she said, before demanding that I "get it out of the house!"

To the chagrin of my neighbors, I scoured nearby backyards with abandon to find prey that could sustain my new pet. The mantis remained my obsession as I watched it eat and grow. I learned where I could find others to join mine, how to distinguish males from females, and quite accidentally, even witnessed its full mating and reproductive process, culminating in the creation of a cocoon-like egg and emergence of hundreds of tiny nymphs the following spring.

Back at school, I watched classmates "play" by angrily crushing insects. Why were they incapable of feeling my same sense of wonder when they spotted a black widow spider, or giant luna moth? This question inspired me to create the Bug Club, a group of peers who showed virtually any interest in, or at least tolerance for, my daily bug expeditions. Not many shared my enthusiasm, but I was pleased that a select few did come to realize bugs might exist for reasons other than to be squashed. The Bug Club was my first realization of how rewarding it was to share my love and curiosity for a topic with others.

Years later, I am using my love of another topic—college football—to cultivate followers of a different sort. I initially created my college football recruiting account on Instagram, @Recruits.CFB, for fun, posting and discussing the latest news and rumors with friends. However, after teaching myself visual design apps like PicsArt, Canva, and Studio, my posts started to gain major traction, accumulating hundreds of new followers each day. Now, I boast one of the premier CFB recruiting accounts on Instagram, which has swelled to over 42,000 followers.

Unlike the Bug Club, these followers are engaged 24/7 and expect new, memorable content every day. "Fan" is short for *fanatic*, and there is no shortage of interest in the top players and their ever-changing recruitments. It's been a multi-year labor of love to keep an eye out for exceptional players and consistently deliver new content. It's also become my first small business venture. I've earned thousands of dollars from those wanting to buy my designs, start affiliated accounts, or pay for promotions to build their own following. As entertaining as it was catching insects in my lunchbox, it's been even more thrilling to hunt daily for new information that informs and influences tens of thousands of people.

Creating the Bug Club and @Recruits.CFB may seem worlds apart, but I have learned that sharing my enthusiasm for a topic with others is a great recipe for satisfaction and success. I know I will always keep searching for spectacular specimens of all kinds, fully expecting to discover much more in this world that intrigues me, and continuing to share and invite others into my discoveries along the way. My hunt for the extraordinary will never end.

Key coaching lesson: Let the passage of time be your friend in an essay. Any anecdote from the past is a form of time travel. But how far in the past? The day you were born? Your childhood? Your recent history? Straight chronology is always the clearest. But flashbacks and time jumps can even work in a short essay. Make sure you test the effects on helpful readers.

Case #5
Wing Place

By Lincoln Murph
(accepted to North Carolina A&T)

Early draft

(675 words)

Growing up, I was always taught the value of giving back whenever possible. My parents instilled in me the importance of empathy, compassion, and humility towards others from a young age. As a kid, they would have me be the one to hand money to the homeless person and teach me to donate a percent of whatever I made to God or charity. Along with lessons of humility and humbleness. As I've grown older, these lessons have only strengthened, and I continue to strive for the betterment of myself and those around me. I make a conscious effort never to look down on those who have less, and never to bow to those who have more. Unfortunately, not everyone shares these values, and some people prey on those who have less, rather than uplifting them.

A few months ago, I witnessed this firsthand. I had just bought a small meal for a random lady who seemed to be struggling, after ordering my own, at a local wing place next to a gas station. I was not thinking much of it other than the fact that I was giving back. Furthermore, I was feeling positive and spirited, seeing how such a small deed could bring a stream of happiness to someone. I remember that some people experience very little positivity in their life, and any amount can be extremely significant for them. However, little did I know that the same positive wave of emotions flowing through me would soon be shattered.

As I waited for my order, I saw another person who was struggling and asking for food. I offered to purchase her an item at the gas station, but she insisted on something from the restaurant. Unfortunately, I had just purchased something for another person, so I had to sincerely apologize to her and was unable to fulfill her request. Upon receiving my food and leaving the restaurant, the same person was still waiting outside. After wishing her a good night, I saw a car wave her over, assuming they would either give her money or food. But I never would have guessed the events that took place next.

A girl with a mask over her face waited for the person to approach the car and then threw food at her while driving off, cursing the person out. The pain I felt at the moment wasn't just mental but physical, as if my body were engulfed in flames. Yet the worst part was the expression on the person's face. I will never forget the empty look on her face, as if she were too numb to feel the pain or anything. At that moment, I immediately apologized to her and took off in my car, driving home, knowing I needed to help this person in any way possible. Mindlessly, I grabbed a bag and subconsciously started pouring food items into it: sandwiches, water, snacks, anything I could find. As my mom came down, we discussed what happened, and she reorganized the bag. We successfully found the homeless person and dropped the food items off. The key idea in that experience was not to reciprocate the negativity that the group of people did to the homeless person. It took my mom a few weeks to really calm me down and open up about the situation.

At the time, I was so infuriated that I couldn't possibly fathom how people could be so heartless to another person. Growing up in a positive environment and learning that I should also be open to all types of people and never dehumanize another person gave me the empathy and kindness that I hold dearly.

Witnessing others who can deride someone who is clearly struggling to just eat and then laugh at them was a thing I could never imagine being possible. Yet, my anger towards them was impacting me. Instead of wasting my time and energy on them, I learned to move on, which is very important in a world where we have people capable of the evil I described.

Analysis by coach Michelle

Lincoln instinctively knew to write his essay on an experience that changed him. While waiting for his order at a wing place near his home, he encountered a person who asked him for food, and then the situation took a shocking turn. It's hard to beat this line for sheer emotion: "The pain I felt at the moment wasn't just mental but physical, as if my body were engulfed in flames." The challenge for Lincoln was to help the reader quickly grasp what was behind that pain and understand what Lincoln did with it. Heartbreaking rage is a bold essay topic, and few writers will feel comfortable taking this kind of risk. Lincoln was all in!

If you're like Lincoln, you're really going to want to avoid unnecessary details. These are even more distracting when the stakes of the story are high. Lincoln enthusiastically dug into revising the essay, and his work was essential to capturing what this moment of fury reveals about him. In the first draft, Lincoln described how his parents instilled in him the value of giving back. This set up why he wanted to help the person who asked him for help.

But "giving back" wasn't the fuel for his heartbreaking rage. Why did Lincoln feel engulfed in flames when he saw strangers being cruel to the hungry person? Lincoln homed in on the idea that sets this essay apart: When vulnerable people are abused, he fights for them, and gets others involved as well. Do you see why this idea is more compelling? "Giving back" is a common value, especially in the United States, the most philanthropic country in the world. While many people give back, few step in to take meaningful, direct action when vulnerable people are harmed. Lincoln is one of these outliers.

An effective coach can help you see where you stand out compared to others. Lincoln overall did a good job of capturing what set off his strong feelings. But his first draft stopped just as it needed to keep going. He agreed to start the action earlier, in the middle of the uncomfortable situation — the stranger asking him for money. New details reveal the economic disparity around him. A cliffhanger gives him the opportunity to provide background, especially about his values. Instead of the cliché of "giving back," Lincoln specifies "empathy, compassion, and humility toward others."

In his revision, Lincoln omitted a description of buying a meal for a different stranger. This act of generosity was slowing down the essay, and Lincoln needed to center on the stranger whose needs were not met. She is the most important supporting character. It's important to ask yourself: What scenes and characters best support my story? Try experimenting by deleting details that aren't 100 percent necessary.

Lincoln did a great job streamlining his narrative. He cleared room to describe the actions he took in his community as a result of this experience. The revised draft distinguishes Lincoln by showing how far he is willing to go for what he believes in. With this new focus, Lincoln achieves the goal of an effective essay: to show something that is important to him and how he thinks about it.

Revised Draft

(627 words)

"I'm sorry, I don't carry cash with me, but I can get you some food," I told the lady who asked me for money outside the wing place. Seeing people in need, less than 10 minutes from my house, is common; they're usually just asking for food or money, or minding their own business.

I could tell from her clothing and dull eyes that she was heavily struggling. She told me she didn't need food, so I went inside and ordered my food, and hoped someone else would help her. After getting my food, I offered once more to purchase her something, but she declined again. Praying for her safety as I approached my car, I spotted a red van approaching her, and as they rolled down the passenger window, I saw a girl wearing a ski mask gesturing for the lady. I was confused as to why she had a ski mask, but I was glad the lady would be getting help. Never could I have predicted what was to come.

My parents instilled in me the importance of empathy, compassion, and humility toward others. As a kid, I would be the one to hand money to a homeless person, and my parents taught me to give a percentage of whatever I made to God or charity. As I've grown older, these lessons have only strengthened, and I make a conscious effort never to look down on those who have less, and never to bow to those who have more. I was used to seeing how even a small deed could bring a stream of happiness to someone because some people experience very little positivity, and any amount can be extremely significant. But I had never witnessed people targeting someone who had nothing for some sort of emotional gain.

Any feelings of compassion were being burnt with feelings of rage as I witnessed the girl, who I'd assumed would help, repeatedly throw chips at the lady. The cruelty continued as they drove off, cursing and laughing at her. I've heard, "You cannot drive out hate with hate, only love can," but at that moment my hate wasn't just a mental pain, but a burning sensation coursing through every inch of my body. Despite my feelings of agony, it surely didn't compare to hers. I knew that deep down she was just barely holding on to the thin line of humanity she had left.

Immediately, I rushed to my car and drove home, where I poured items into a bag for the lady. My mother calmed me down, and we logically prepared a gift bag, safely going back and giving it to the lady. Remembering the lifeless look on the lady's face is what fuels me to fight for those who have no one in their corner. Thinking about evil is vastly different from seeing evil from my own eyes, and holding on to the memory of their hate would just further consume me. Instead, I needed to open my mind and realize there were two victims in the situation: the lady and the group of people.

Beacon United, a group that my friend and I started, is meant to help educate our community about people who are victims of dehumanization and about the people who prey on them. Homeless people aren't the plague, and instead of avoiding them, we should be helping. Down the street shouldn't foster such injustice like that. I want to spread respect to everyone, no matter if they drive a BMW or stand up against the wall of the wing place and ask people for money. This event opened my eyes to the reality that helping people is important, but uniting people in respect is how we can make the greatest difference.

* * *

Key coaching lessons: Even if you are not working with a coach, you can find the focus of your story by asking yourself this question: What is my essay really about? If you can answer that question, it will help you figure out what to add to the story. As important, or more important, is the ability to see the scenes, people, and details that distract your reader from the main point or most powerful emotion. Think of it as a way of coaching yourself.

Case #6
The Sand Dollar

By Allison McQuiston
(accepted to Colorado State University)

We are not publishing the entire original version of this story for two reasons: It was written not as a college admissions essay, but for an assignment in a high school writing class. Also, that early version was almost four times the length of the final version below, more than two thousand words. Any teacher could tell that the original version was exceptionally well done. It had a kind of literary flair, an exemplary use of language, and a thematic sensitivity that would mark the student as ready for college.

The story described her childhood visits to a beachy island, lyrical memories of natural beauty, innocence, and a playful peace of mind. Here is an excerpt:

First Draft

I was practically raised on this island, with its poorly paved roads and three empty stores. When I was young, it seemed as big as all of America. I could run and play for miles on the endless beach. It was nothing but sandy flip-flops, greasy sunscreen, and racing the tide to protect our precious sand castles. It was laughter over game night, and thrilling movies on rainy days. It was a haven.

Analysis by coach Michelle

This writer started with a long essay that she had written for school. It's always great to have existing content, but it can be challenging to find the shorter, personal essay hiding inside. It can be like walking into a comfortable and familiar room and being able to see how to renovate it for another use. Professional writers and editors do this all the time, of course. The essay becomes a short story. It grows into a novel. Shrinks into a screenplay. Grows into a Netflix series.

The writer and I began by reviewing the long essay, looking for what was special in it. I wrote this note to the writer: "This is tremendous writing. I don't have much criticism to give, so I'll tell you what I like. I love how you structured the story by moving back and forth in time. I also enjoy how you set the scene with your descriptions. There is a lot of depth in your reflections. Ending with the sand dollars is such an interesting choice. It leaves the reader thinking about how we remember the past, and how we hold our memories. You should be really proud of this!"

What she needed was a focus. Not a scanning of many different images of her youthful visits to the beach. All of those beach scenes and anecdotes led in the end to two pages in which the writer describes her search for sand dollars, and the shifting meaning of the shells to her over time. It turned out to be the perfect focus for an essay of up to 650 words. This essay is a good example of using a single object of meaning to show what is important to you and how you think about it.

The writer had to be willing to jettison most of the first essay to get to the final. She had earned an A on that essay and had to put that out of her mind to make the new version. To find the new version, she had to remove herself from the first. She had to come to see it as fertile ground to plant something new and maybe even more meaningful. And carving a new essay out of an old one can be much harder than writing two separate pieces.

By showing how you think, you will likely show how you learn. This writer shows how new information about the environment changed her view of collecting sand dollars. To embody that change, the writer has to be the central character in the story, without distractions.

Revised Draft

(641 words)

At the age of five, I glanced from shell shard to broken shell shard until I saw a familiar silver form resting half-buried in sand. Squealing in excitement as any child would, I squatted low and eased the sand dollar from the beach's grasp. A small crack reached precariously along one edge, but I still marveled at the beauty. After all, the crack was just another unique design, was it not?

I stumbled towards my mom, peering into her cupped hands filled with an abundance of nearly identical sand dollars. "Can you hold it for me?"

"Are you sure you need this one as well? You have many others and this one has a crack in it."

"I'm sure," I replied, tucking the new addition tightly among the others.

"There sure are a lot of sand dollars this year, don't you think?" my dad suggested, looking around at the beach that was abnormally littered with the gray disks.

"Yeah! It's awesome," I exclaimed, before skipping off to collect more.

As I grew older, I couldn't believe that the younger me had been so happy to find so much death. I now turned a silver disk over in my hand, tracing the dark gray pattern with a long, delicate finger. Its simplicity was captivating, and I found I was holding my breath in the presence of such a fragile object.

Shells, I now know, don't materialize to fill our pockets. They were once living creatures with stories and pasts. We collect their alluring skeletons as trinkets, not thinking twice of the life they once supported. How ironic that something so pretty bore the markings of death.

I was left to wonder what had strangled the life out of so many sea creatures that year long ago. Some chemical in the water, most likely, had left the scattered remains on the sand. But the shells weren't just discarded corpses; they told stories with every crack and worn surface.

I don't know how to make sense of my joyous childhood memory because this new truth left a sour taste in my mouth. When you're five, the cracks of a shell do little to taint its worth, but now that the truth completely dimmed the pure light of that memory? No. I still appreciate the pride I had felt with each shell. I admire how the sand dollar remains to prove to the world that this creature had lived, and maybe as a trinket, someone will remember them. They may be cracked and faded, but more than any pretty pattern they bear, shells hold importance and meaning that is truly breathtaking. The dark truth, I have decided, is not a death sentence to the happy memory, but a crack in its shell that adds a deeper elegance.

Now, as I reflect on those times, I find truth from both perspectives. The image of beauty, in the eye of a child, is as simple as what brings them joy, while maturity allows you to appreciate both the surface beauty and the story of how it came to be. My memories of summers spent pacing the beach are as delicate and intricate as the shells I have scavenged. They're beautiful, fragile remnants of my childhood innocence. Their cracks and chips might scare some people off, might lead to them being tossed back on the sand, but my shells, my memories, captivate me because of their scars. I don't want time to dull my view of the world, or to start tossing shells back to the waves because they aren't perfect. I treasure my blissful youth, my growing body of knowledge, and the stories that lie beneath the surface of both.

I tucked the sand dollar safely in my pocket. It was pretty when laced with oblivion, but it became beautiful when bearing the truth of its past.

Most important coaching lesson: To get from more than 2,000 words to 650, find a focus and use it to cut elements in the essay that do not support it. Donald Murray writes that "brevity comes from selection and not compression." Roy Peter Clark writes: "Prune the big limbs before you shake out the dead leaves."

Part X

Learn and Inspire

From this section you can learn:

* What a truly great student essay looks like
* How the best coaches work — help you can share with parents and teachers

ONE FINAL ESSAY TO READ AND APPRECIATE

There are young writers who can take the craft of the personal essay and transform it into a work of art. I have saved the essay that follows as the final example of how well-crafted, how creative, how moving a story by a high school student can be. Don't be intimidated by its quality. Instead, take it in, read my appreciation that follows, and think about what you can learn from it.

Leap of Faith

By Asher Montgomery
(accepted to Harvard University, 2023)

(645 words)

The sky was pitch black on Cotopaxi at 2 a.m. My headlamp barely lit the ice ahead of me. The snow turned my braided hair to ice, and every few steps I stopped to suck breath, like I was hyperventilating.

"I can't do this anymore," I thought.

As if he was reading my mind, the guide shouted down to me.

"Asher, you're suffering because you are thinking about your pain," he hollered. "Go to your happy place."

Then I felt a tug on the rope tied to my waist, telling me to keep walking against the wind, against the sleet, against the snow.

I was too exhausted to cry, or to find a happy place. I could only think, "What am I doing here?"

I only had myself to blame. Climbing the 19,347-foot glacial volcano was my idea.

It was my idea because, the year before, on a hike in Alaska, I happened to look to my right and see Denali's breathtaking peak and think, "That is where I want to be." And because a few months later the Internet told me that Cotopaxi was great for beginner mountaineers. And, finally, because my dad found cheap flights to Ecuador for the summer of 2021.

I also thought it was something my brother would have liked to do.

Before Cotopaxi, before Alaska, and before my little brother died by suicide, we loved to go on hikes.

Long hikes.

For months at a time, we would camp and wake as the birds started chirping and walk along the rugged Appalachian Trail. Together we'd count the salamanders by the stream as my dad filtered water. We invented our own language—snails were "snake-cars," birds were "up-dogs," fellow hikers were "moving rocks."

It wasn't all fun. When I hadn't showered in nine days and climbed into my sleeping bag like some kind of stink burrito. Or when we had to walk miles in the dark to make it to camp. But my siblings and I always left the trail feeling freer than we ever had, proud of ourselves and closer to each other.

We dragged my sister along on the Ecuador trip, but after three tough hikes to get acclimated to the altitude, she decided to opt out of the last climb:

Cotopaxi. I tried to convince her otherwise, but she made the right call, for herself.

And my dad, he wasn't doing much better than I was. His silence was a sign to me that he was in just as much pain.

He told me later that he only kept going because I refused to turn back.

I wanted more than anything at that moment to make it to the top because it never crossed my mind that we wouldn't make it, and because I hoped I might be able to feel my little brother at the top.

But as the wind picked up and the air got thinner in the bone-biting cold, our legs grew exhausted and still hadn't reached the steepest part.

The guide told us there that it was too dangerous to continue.

I finally started crying, tears of relief and disappointment.

We turned around. It was still dark. On the descent, the sun began to rise, lighting the clouds that surrounded the warrior mountain.

We stopped for a moment at the signal of the guide. He began pulling the rope out to give it slack. He told me to wait until the rope pulled to begin walking again. He walked out in front until I couldn't see him. When it was my turn, I reached a gap in the ice. A crevasse. I knew what to do. I stepped back, ran forward, and put all of the energy I had into a leap.

Soaring over the bottomless crevasse, I understood,
somewhere in this struggle, that pain and uncertainty
are not an end.

WHAT I SEE

Of all the essays in this book, this one touches me the deepest. I have known the writer, Asher Montgomery, since she
was a child. A multitalented young woman from a creative
and adventurous family, Asher has been a musician, an activist, and a strong writer since she was in middle school. When
I learned she had applied to Harvard, it did not surprise me,
although I knew that many high-achieving students apply to
Harvard and find themselves rejected.

When I read this essay, I understood why she was
accepted and now, in her first year, has found a place at the
Harvard Crimson, the school's famous student publication.
(Which, by the way, has published its own collection of outstanding admissions essays.)

As Asher was still in high school, trying to figure out her
future, she and her family suffered an unimaginable tragedy,
the death of her younger brother. If you have read her essay,
you can begin to appreciate how skillfully she handled this
traumatic experience as an element in her story.

Instead of describing the tragedy in all its painful detail,
Asher makes the powerful decision to understate a devastating event that could easily have dominated her narrative.

Understatement is a powerful tool in storytelling. When a story is lighthearted, as several of the essays in this book are, overstatement, even exaggeration, may work the best. But in a case such as Asher's, less turns out to be so much more.

She encases news of the tragedy in a journey of aspiration and desperation, filled with descriptive language that builds a powerful narrative. Stories need characters, scenes, settings, and chronologies, and this one has all of those. It also is built around a symbol, of sorts, perhaps what we might call an archetype; she uses the act of climbing a mountain as a metaphor for overcoming obstacles and achieving knowledge.

In the myths of ancient Greece, Sisyphus repeatedly pushes a rock up a hill, only to see it roll back every time. Moses receives the commandments from the top of Mount Sinai. Mount Olympus was where the Greek gods hung out. Even in our common language we talk about the hills we have to climb, and the glory that comes from reaching the top.

Asher proves the wisdom of my high school teacher who told us that in good writing "a symbol need not be a cymbal." In other words, no need to force-feed meaning into the mouths of readers. Instead, the meaning reveals itself in one final moment, when Asher is fully prepared to take a literal leap of faith: a jump across a crevasse that leads to an uncertain but hopeful future.

The story reveals so much about Asher's character: her intelligence, resilience, physical courage, and sensitivity. This is the kind of person I would want to join my community of teaching and learning.

It is important for me to add that you should not feel

intimidated by the unique elements on display in this essay. You may not have experienced such a terrible personal loss. You may not have been born into a family that has the resources to undertake exciting adventures.

But you have your own experiences, and your own stories about loss, hope, family, aspiration, failure, and triumph. You don't need to write the most dramatic essay in the class to get you where you want to go — only one that is revealing and true. You can do it.

COACHING THE STUDENT AND THE ESSAY: A GUIDE FOR ALL HELPERS

We have seen the good effects when writing coaches and helpers work with student writers to find what works and what needs work in a personal essay. The craft of coaching or editing is not just operating on a broken text or performing an autopsy on a cadaver. Coaching takes two kinds of intelligence: (1) the literary skill to see the unfulfilled potential in a text, and (2) the emotional intelligence to motivate and guide a writer to improve the text through revision.

Michelle Hiskey is such a writing coach. She has proven with students and professionals to have the "hardware" and the "software." She listens, suggests, listens again, evaluates, shares, motivates, and keeps listening, through draft after draft. After she shared with me the results of her coaching, I asked her to share her coaching process.

You will read it below. Classroom teachers can use these strategies; so can counselors, tutors, other writers, coaches, and, yes, even parents.

The Essay Coaching Lane:
Finding It, Staying in It, Thriving in It

By Michelle Hiskey

So where is home—your comfort zone and the writer's—when you're coaching a student on their college essay—perhaps for the first or only time? So much is riding on this! You want to avoid too much guidance, while offering feedback that works.

Since coaching my first student in 2011, I have become more comfortable with my process, and now I want to describe it to you. What to do, and what not to do.

In essay coaching, less is more. A lot more. And because my mentor Roy Peter Clark has taught me lots of writing tools, I'll offer these twenty-two practical strategies to help you coach a successful essay.

GETTING STARTED

1. Be invited. Don't impose support on a student, even if they need it badly. Your relationship will be much better if they initiate. Try to meet at a time and place where they are most comfortable.

2. Ask the student to set as "SMART" a goal as possible.
"Getting the essay done" is a task, not a goal. SMART goals are specific, measurable, attainable, realistic, and time-sensitive. A typical goal might be "I want to finish a draft of my Common App essay by September 1, and I want to make myself stand out by what I write about and how I write it." You will want to keep the goal top of mind as you coach.

As a coach, I set my own goal, too. It's always the same: "When you hit submit, I want you to feel that this essay is as good as you can make it. Your essay is one of the few things that you control as you apply for college. After that point, what the college decides is not in your control." This helps create a safe container for our work together.

3. Understand the difficulty and pressure of the task.
The student likely perceives that the essay will make or break their acceptance into college, even if that may not be true. With so many great essays online, your student may feel insecure about finding a topic that captures who they are and choosing the best way to write about it. Their friend group may be adding to the stress, especially if they are aiming to meet the same application deadlines. Your student may also lack instruction and experience in writing a personal essay, and now they have to do so within a word count by a certain deadline. A great coach is attuned to these pressures and looking for ways to alleviate, not add to them.

4. Understand the target. The college essay shows two things: something that the student cares about, and how that student thinks about it. A great essay allows the college admissions reader to hear the student's authentic voice and picture the student in this moment. Hopefully the college will learn something about the student that is not shared elsewhere on the application. A memorable essay often includes some introspection and the desire to grow. These are your targets.

5. Tailor your coaching style to the student. When a student first comes to me for coaching, I always ask them to describe someone who helped them improve at something difficult. What was that person like? The student usually talks about a teacher or coach who motivated them to keep going in a certain way. Maybe it was through constant encouragement, or by consistently raising the bar. Or humor. Always a deep sense of caring. Their answer helps you understand what kind of coaching works for this student.

CHOOSING THE TOPIC

Don't go into coaching thinking that it's your responsibility to determine the best topic. Only the student can do that. Their best topic is already inside them. Your job is to help them find it. Here are some ways to do that.

6. Corral all the ideas. Ideally a student has multiple topics in mind for the essay, and the coach helps them see which one best serves their goal. Of course, some students struggle to find a single topic. Coming up with topics requires that you keep the conversation going. Some questions that help get students thinking: What is the story behind your name? Do you have a nickname? What is a story about yourself that makes you laugh? What's a time when you felt most awkward and what did you learn from it? Is there an important relationship that changed you?

7. Observe the student's body language as they describe each topic. Does their face light up about nuclear fission or anime? Do they pale at the idea of writing about a life-changing car accident? *The best topic usually is the one that the student is most excited to write about.* This desire acts as an engine to motivate them through the tough work of drafts and revisions.

If the student's demeanor doesn't provide any clues, use their goal to test each topic. Examples: "Lego competitions are pretty common for kids who want to become engineers, so how could you distinguish yourself in that story?" Or "It doesn't seem like too many high school seniors know how to make a roux from scratch. What do you think?"

8. Avoid self-defeating topics. A coach needs to guide the student away from any topic that harms their chance of college acceptance. Confessing to being chronically distracted, for instance, could be the start of a successful essay about how a student learned to overcome this challenge, but it's self-defeating as an entire essay, because attentiveness is a core skill needed in higher education. Resist any topic that depicts the student as privileged, entitled, or a person of questionable morals. Legal trouble and love interests are rarely good essay topics.

9. Build in time to choose among topics. After discussing the merits of each, and keeping the student's goal in mind, give the student time to choose. Ideally this is a specific span before the next coaching session, and the student knows that they are in charge of this decision and that you believe in them and support the topic of their choice. The next session will be focused on structuring the essay around the selected topic.

COACHING ESSAY STRUCTURE

Once the student has decided on the topic, what is the arc of the story they are going to tell? One of the most gratifying opportunities in essay coaching is helping a student structure the essay. The most natural type of college essay to write is the narrative essay, with a beginning, middle, and end. Because humans are wired to tell stories in this format, I urge students and coaches to use it whenever possible.

Let's imagine that the student wants to write about the time they tried breakdancing and split their pants. You know from the previous coaching session that they experienced humiliation, but they now laugh at that memory. Here's how you could help the student structure an essay like this.

10. Use a timeline. A narrative essay must include why and how the student changes. This change is going to happen over time, so a timeline is a handy tool. Always remember that the student is the expert on what happened when, and why it is important to them; the coach is helping plot the important turning points on the timeline.

The coach and student in this example use these six common turning points on the timeline to show the student's growth:

- Student before event (breakdancing attempt) — Why did they try this?
- Student during event (breakdancing) — Who was watching? Where was this? What happened?
- Student consequences after event (public humiliation) — Make sure to describe the lowest point.
- Student growth (learning to laugh at themselves) — Transformation is the heart of the essay, so the student will want to spend the most time describing how and why they changed.
- Student shares or tests new knowledge — Transformation is more believable when the student tests what they have learned, or shares it with someone else. This is a brief anecdote.
- Student goes forward — how does this experience prepare them for the future, in college or in pursuit of an academic or professional goal?

11. Identify the hook(s). Most students know about (and can be obsessed with) their essay "hook." This is essentially the compelling lead that lures the reader into the story. It's also important because the first paragraphs of the essay may be the only part that gets read at a college that receives a large number of applications. In a college essay, there's no upside to throat-clearing (starting the story slowly).

To identify potential hooks, look for moments in the story where the student faces a question. Often the best hook is the most compelling question, and it's not always at the start of the timeline. But that's OK! It can still appear at the start of the essay.

In this example, the student determines that their most compelling dilemma was having to walk into school after this public humiliation. That becomes the hook. Can you start an essay in the middle of the timeline? Yes, by incorporating a flashback.

So the structure now looks like this:

- Starting hook: Returning to school after public humiliation was the lowest point.
- [Flashback:] Before breakdancing attempt, why did they try this? During breakdancing, who was watching? Where was this? What happened?
- [End flashback, return to scene of walking into school]
- Student learns to laugh at themselves, and describes how and why they changed.
- Student shares a brief anecdote about how they tested or shared what they have learned.
- Ending: Student describes how this experience prepares them for the future, in college or in pursuit of an academic or professional goal.

This can now serve as the outline of the student's essay.

12. Ask the student to use the outline to draft the essay.
The outline or plan is the student's best guess at how to
tell the story with the information they have so far. Go
over the plan together to make sure that the student feels it is
generally accurate and makes sense. Change anything that
needs to be changed. You may want to ask if anything big
is left out, but tread lightly; writers often think an essay
needs every detail, but the main objective is to get the *right*
details.

**13. Urge the student to ignore the word count (at least
at first).** The goal at this point is for the student to have
maximum freedom to tell all of the story. Encourage them
to write scenes with sensory details, and to err on the side of
too many. Assure them that they will be able to reduce the
essay to the desired length in the revising stage of the
process.

**14. Remind them that they are writing to a supportive
audience.** Some students mistakenly think that the admissions officer is looking for any imperfection in their story as
an excuse to disqualify them, as if a magistrate judge were on
the other end, ready to bring down a gavel of rejection. But
that's not the case! Readers of college admission essays
want to feel a connection with your student and invite them
into the incoming class. Remind your student that the reader
wants to read a great essay that only the student can write. A
writer who can relax in the knowledge that their reader is
supportive is most likely to create their best work.

COACHING THE DRAFT

This is where some students start with a coach: they already have a draft of their essay, and they need guidance on finishing it. Or sometimes the first draft is incomplete because the student got stuck. Usually there are issues!

15. Ask for the student's diagnosis. Withhold immediate feedback! First, ask the student what kind of help they think they need. What do they like about this draft? Where did they experience difficulties? Is anything missing? Affirm their work and ownership of the essay. Prioritize their observations in your feedback.

16. Give a movie of your reading. I like to read the draft aloud to the student so we can hear the words and notice what is happening in the draft and what isn't. Then I use a technique that writing coach Chip Scanlan calls giving a movie of my reading: I narrate my experience of reading what the student has written — line by line, describing my growing understanding of (and maybe some confusion about) the story. In the hypothetical breakdancing draft, I can imagine telling the student how much I love their description of the facial expressions of the crowd. I'd also note that the terms "cyphers" and "freezes" might be understandable in context, but let's make sure to define them in the final revision.

This type of feedback is effective because it focuses on clarifying the story, not nitpicking about the writing. Don't underestimate how personal the personal essay is to a student. Almost nothing is less useful (and potentially hurtful) than a vague "I don't like this." Always craft the feedback so that the essay is moving toward the student's goals.

If you want to skip the movie of your reading, you can assess the draft this way: Does it sound like the student? Does it reflect who the student is in this moment? Does it share something not likely to be revealed elsewhere on the application? Does it sound like someone who is ready for college? Remember the compliment sandwich: Focus on something you really like about it and make that your first piece of feedback, then a few suggestions for improvement, then an overall positive comment.

17. Suggest, don't edit. The feedback, like the essay, belongs to the student. Respect what they decide to do with it. Suggestions (not edits) on Google Docs, or perhaps on sticky notes, give them the option to accept or reject feedback.

18. Work together on filling in incomplete or missing information. Students often skip over the critical part of the story where their transformation happens. That's usually where you may need to urge them to go deeper. If, for example, they are telling the story of a time they faced a difficult decision, ask them questions like these: What other options could they have chosen? How did their choice change them? What did they learn from the experience? These details reveal what is important to the student and how they think. This transformation *is* their essay. If length is an issue, other parts can be condensed.

19. A great ending is essential, and usually difficult. Even seasoned professional writers have difficulty writing endings! I advise students to bring all their authority to the ending of the essay, to "bring the hammer down" and really own what they have experienced and what it means to them.

Strengthening the ending in the early draft also gives the student a clear finish line as well as a boost of confidence. In the breakdancing example, the student describes how the debacle prepared them for handling embarrassing setbacks or failures in the future, whether in college or in pursuit of an academic or professional goal.

An ending doesn't have to be long; a short paragraph can be plenty. And if you can help the student avoid sounding like a Hallmark card, the essay will automatically stand out.

COACHING REVISION/S

20. Don't start trimming too early. There's no point in editing down an essay if it's missing information that is essential to understanding the student's story. Generally, the student needs one revision on their own and maybe some additional collaboration (as described in the previous point). As the student describes what happened and what point they want to make, I often take rough notes for the student to use in the revision. (It can be revelatory for a student to see how their spoken words can serve as essay text. This is part of my core belief that if a student can tell their story aloud, they can write an essay about it.) If necessary, repeat steps 16, 17, and 18 until the essay has everything it needs.

21. Trim around the transformation. Sometimes the essay draft will be quite a bit longer than the word limit (650 words for the Common App, for example). Don't worry! It can be helpful to review the original structure of the essay for the essential elements, then help the student trim around them. Students often spend more time and words than they need setting up the transformation.

A good way to coach for edits is to suggest specific deletions, or highlight sections that need to be condensed. Often, I work separately from the student in this stage and explain my suggestions using comments in the shared Google Doc.

This is where you can bear down (but not too much) on grammar suggestions and point out unnecessary adverbs and adjectives, as well as random capitalization. Look for redundancies.

It is normal for an essay written by a high school student to have some run-on sentences, awkward uses of punctuation, and other grammar imperfections. A college essay is unlikely to be perfect.

A final edit needs to ensure that nothing important is left out and that the student verifies the accuracy of everything in the essay. Have them read aloud to catch any extra or missing words.

22. Wrap up with confidence and celebration. Once the final edit is complete, there's usually a lot of relief, especially if the submission deadline is close. Don't miss the chance to celebrate with your student the specific aspects of their essay and hard work that you admire. Telling them that they did a good job is the bare minimum here. This is a moment to give them something specific to boost their confidence and understanding of themselves as a writer.

AVOID

- Worrying that your student won't get in because of their essay
- Pressuring the student to write about a particular topic, especially a painful one (If you are a parent, be particularly wary of pressuring them into a topic that reflects positively on you or on a childhood experience.)
- Ghostwriting the essay

A Grading Rubric to Help You
Judge Your Own Essay

As a final bit of learning, it might be helpful for you to know the word *rubric*. It comes from the Latin meaning "marked in red." A rubric is a kind of grading system that helps readers evaluate the quality of a piece of writing. Rather than just grade a paper as a whole, a rubric lists the elements that make it good and gives a numerical value for each. In the rubric I have created for you, I have chosen ten categories, each one on a subjective scale of 1–10. I am not saying this is how your essay will be assessed. Instead, I am offering it to you as a summary of some key lessons in this book and as a checklist of things you may want to pay attention to.

1. Adhere to the prompt. The best prompts are open doors, not tiny fissures. No one is trying to trick you into tripping over the prompt. Show evidence that you understand the prompt and that you have chosen it with purpose.

2. Make creative use of the prompt. Think of the prompt as a launching pad. Don't be afraid to be playful or to surprise the reader with your choices. Facing a challenge, for example, can apply to climbing a mountain or winning a Halloween costume contest. The prompt should help you write something (a) important, (b) interesting, or (c) both.

3. Reveal a distinctive voice. Read drafts of your story aloud. Have others read them to you. Make a list of how you want to "sound" to the reader: scholarly, creative, modest. Don't try to sound like something you are not. Be yourself— or maybe be a little better than your normal self.

4. Find a sharp focus. Focus is the heart of the writing process. It means that your essay is about several aspects of one thing. Not one aspect of several things. If you have many talents, for example, you will be tempted to sneak them all in. Share your passion or your intense curiosity in as direct a statement as you can: "I am a girl who wants to be an astrophysicist. Learn to live with it."

5. Tell a compelling story. The best essays are not always pure stories from beginning to end. But most good ones have story elements: anecdotes, small scenes, interesting characters, a bit of dialogue. A story is not a list of your achievements. It's taking readers by the hand and letting them watch you cross the finish line for victory, or fall on your face, crushing your dreams.

6. Include interesting details. Details will bring your story to life and reveal your character. Those details may be about you, that you were born with eleven toes. Or they can be things you notice in the world, like the priest who has a Beatles logo tattooed on his arm. Without specific details, an essay can sound abstract and general.

7. Show an interest in words. You can't expand your writing vocabulary in a week, but you can always do a better job with the language you have. You don't have to use fancy or technical words, such as *polydactyl*, meaning "having one or more extra fingers or toes." It might be just as well to use your aunt Polly, who interested you in biology. You can always use a thesaurus, a treasure chest that lists synonyms, words with the same meaning. But I don't use a thesaurus to learn new words, only to remind me of words I may have forgotten. See how I slipped in the phrase "treasure chest" up there? You know that phrase. It makes my definition of *thesaurus* more interesting.

8. Make sure parts fit together. The best essays have a structure, an organization, a thoughtful order that builds meaning. Does the essay have a clear beginning, middle, and end? Do they fit together so there are no extra parts? Is a story developed? Does meaning grow?

9. Offer evidence of your academic interest. Many students go to college without a clear idea of who they are and what they want to become. A good education will help you construct a productive future. I have worked with two young women, one who wanted to become an astrophysicist, and another who was passionate about sailing. It was important to Emme to have lots of science in her essay, and for Rosie to describe what competitive sailing has taught her about risk and reward. Evidence of your knowledge and interest helps build your case.

10. Inspect and correct. Is there evidence that you have checked the text carefully, on your own and, when appropriate, with the help of others? Are words spelled correctly? Is the essay free of common grammatical or other language mistakes? Have facts been checked? Have needless words been eliminated? Is the format clean, clear, and readable, with paragraphs short enough to create helpful white space?

Bonus: The "It Factor." For extra credit. There are intangible qualities that attract the interest of readers. The It Factor refers to that undefinable quality that makes a person or some form of expression seem special. Another good word for this is "spirit." Does this essay show a writer with spirit, someone who truly wants to join this community on our campus?

ACKNOWLEDGMENTS

The top of this list of thanks goes to Talia Krohn, my new editor at Little, Brown, who pitched the idea to me. Given the success of my book *Writing Tools*, Talia imagined we could publish such a book of tools for high school students working on their personal essays for college. After twenty books, I did not think I had another writing book in me, but Talia proved me wrong.

This is my eighth book since 2006 with Little, Brown. The first seven were acquired and edited by Tracy Behar, who turned me from an aspiring writer into an author. The matchmaker of that fruitful relationship was my agent, Jane Dystel. I could say that I love my agent, which I do, but even more telling: I believe my agent can beat up your agent!

I must heap thanks upon book artist Keith Hayes. Even during the time he wasn't working for LB, he volunteered his creativity and artistry to design the imaginative cover art for eight books in a row. The amazing things Keith can see in the image of a simple pencil! Please, dear readers, once again judge my latest book by its cover.

Every daring writer—from student to professional—needs a good safety net. My helpers include two fine writers and great copy editors, Betsy Uhrig and Kathryn Rogers. They save me, time and again, from my false assumptions and my flabby verbs.

My first book, *Free to Write: A Journalist Teaches Young Writers*, was published in 1985. It describes my experiences teaching writing as a volunteer in my daughters' public schools. Those fourth and fifth graders are now in their forties and fifties. Many have stayed in touch, reminding me of the power of early education in reading and writing. I am grateful for the heroic work—in the face of vicious political opposition—of language arts teachers and school librarians. They are my teachers, too.

In 2012, the Poynter Institute wondered if we could offer a program for high school students on how to write a good personal essay, to help them get into the college of their choice. My partner in this effort was Kelly McBride, now a vice president at Poynter and currently the public editor for National Public Radio. The program did not last long, but Kelly and I have saved and grown our resources on the topic. You can find them throughout the book. Thanks to Neil Brown and all my other Poynter colleagues.

Thanks to my young colleague Mallary Tenore Tarpley and her family. I met Mal when she was a student at Providence College and watched her grow into a true professional as a writer, writing teacher, and author.

This book would have been impossible without the contributions of feature writer and writing coach Michelle Hiskey. I knew that she was a good coach — she actually helped me with my golf game. But she was able to provide telling examples and lessons that enrich this book, along with great advice for anyone who wants to help a student write better.

I am lucky to live in St. Petersburg, Florida, which has become over the last four decades a City of Writers. Thanks to all my colleagues at the *Tampa Bay Times*. Thanks to the great women of Tombolo Books. Thanks to the folks at the Catalyst and the St. Petersburg Press. Special thanks to all the coffee shop owners and servers who keep us creative types fueled and ready to go, each and every morning.

Thanks to my brothers, Vincent and Ted. To my daughters, Emily, Lauren, and Alison, and to their extended families. Thanks, most of all, to Karen for giving me the dining room to turn into my home office during quarantine. I did not think I could write a book staring at her knickknack collection, but I did!

Permissions

Special thanks go to writers Sam French, Emme Slaughter, Charley Daly, and Asher Montgomery. I have known them — and their supportive families — since they were children. It has been a pleasure to see them grow into their college work and beyond. Without their permission to publish and analyze their work, I could not have written this book.

My dear friend Mallary Tenore Tarpley invited me to visit, via video call, her writing class at the University of Texas at Austin. It was a class of first-year students, which meant they'd had the recent experience of writing their way into college. I described this book project, inviting them to share their high school essays. To my delight and surprise, seven students sent me their work with permission to use it in the book. Their generosity, and their diversity, will be of help to many young writers.

My collaborator on this book, Michelle Hiskey, has coached many students in creating their personal essays. Seven of them have given us permission to reprint not only the final version of their essays, but early versions as well. These case studies on both coaching and revision, with before and after examples, offer special tools to our readers.

It was wonderful to catch up to two writers whose stories appeared as Youth Radio pieces more than a decade ago. Sasha Black and Brandon McFarland both eagerly gave their permission after we found them. Special thanks go to Rebecca Martin from Youth Media, who helped us find Sasha and Brandon, and who gave us not only permission, but encouragement to use these essays.

INDEX

239

About the Author

Roy Peter Clark taught his first writing class to college students in 1974, which gives him an honest half-century working on his craft as a writer, reader, and teacher. By some accounts, he has become America's writing coach, devoted to creating a nation of writers. A Ph.D. in medieval literature, he is widely considered the most influential writing teacher in the rough-and-tumble world of journalism. With a deep background in traditional news media, Clark has illuminated the discussion of writing on the internet. He has gained fame by teaching writing to children, and he has nurtured winners of the Pulitzer Prize. He is a teacher who writes, and a writer who teaches.

Since 1977, Clark has taught writing at the Poynter Institute, a school for journalism and democracy in St. Petersburg, Florida, considered among the most prominent such teaching institutions in the world. He graduated from Providence College with a degree in English and earned his Ph.D. from Stony

Brook University. In 2017 he was given an honorary degree from his alma mater and invited to deliver the commencement address at Providence's centennial celebration. During that speech, he played and sang a Beatles song.

In 1977 he was hired by the *St. Petersburg Times* (now the *Tampa Bay Times*) as one of America's first writing coaches and worked with the American Society of News Editors to improve newswriting nationwide. He has taught writing at news organizations, schools, businesses, nonprofits, and government agencies in more than forty states and on five continents.

Among his clients at Poynter: the *New York Times*, the *Washington Post*, National Public Radio, *National Geographic*, *USA Today*, CNN, Gannett, Microsoft, IBM, the US Department of Health and Human Services, Disney, AAA, the United Nations, the World Bank, and countless colleges and universities.

Clark has authored or edited twenty-one books about writing, reading, language, and journalism. Some have been translated in Spanish, Danish, German, Arabic, Chinese, and Russian. Humorist Dave Barry has said of him, "Roy Peter Clark knows more about writing than anybody I know who is not currently dead."

Clark lives with his family in St. Petersburg, Florida, where two writing contests have been named in his honor. He writes regular columns for the *Tampa Bay Times*, where he is a favorite of readers who still like to hold paper in their hands.

About Contributor Michelle Hiskey

Michelle aspires to be to writing what coach Dawn Staley is to basketball: a writer and reporter of high achievement who helps bring out the best writing in others. Michelle's professional writing career began in high school as a stringer for her local paper. She earned journalism and golf scholarships to Duke University and spent twenty-two years reporting for the *Atlanta Journal-Constitution*. A mother of two adult daughters, she was part of a Pulitzer Prize finalist team and won Cox Newspapers' Feature Writer of the Year. She trained at the Poynter Institute in writing before becoming an invited speaker. Now leading her own writing firm in Decatur, Georgia, Michelle is immensely grateful for a profession that constantly challenges her. Coaching young writers on their essays is her joy. Students and families that would like her direct help on essays can reach her at michelle.hiskey@gmail.com.